GREAT AMERICANS SPEAK

GREAT
AMERICANS SPEAK

Facsimiles of Original Editions selected and annotated

by JOHN E. POMFRET

THE WARD RITCHIE PRESS

1968

Contents

Preface

SINCE THE STAMP ACT *remonstrances of 1765 which foretold the Revolution against England, millions upon millions of words have been spoken and written about the genesis and destiny of the American Republic.*

The selections in this volume may not be the greatest spoken or written upon the subject but it would be an understatement to label them merely "representative."

Always the Republic has had to confront crises and grave problems. Today we are told again and again that our heritage and our way of life must be defended. But the spokesmen presented here are more positive and more constructive in character. They look ever forward, with confidence and with boldness.

Whatever the problem, whatever the age, Americans have spoken out. They were unafraid. Let us not forget that, when delivered, many of these statements of public policy were greeted with derision or scorn, indifference or neglect. Even today men will differ with some of them. But, so long as America is a land of free men, they will continue to be read.

Since everyone is familiar with the Declaration of Independence, the Constitution, and the Emancipation Proclamation, these have been omitted. The selections included here are well known for they are referred to almost daily in the press, but they are known in name rather than in substance. Since they are not so readily available, the object of this volume is to give them a wider currency.

If these great documents have any quality in common it is that of simplicity. These men were speaking in all sincerity. Some were pleading unpopular or even losing causes in behalf of what they considered to be the public good. Few were professional writers or orators but without exception their expressions were forthright and vigorous.

The printing and format of the original documents were plain, if not poor. In the early years of the Republic paper was expensive, thus the type-size was small and the page was crowded. The final page of Washington's Farewell Address was a masterpiece of economy. The later addresses originated in the government printing office or were sponsored by party headquarters. Here again, the object was to produce the largest number of copies at the cheapest rate. Thus some of our most important pronouncements are represented by some of the poorest exhibitions of the printer's craft. Yet in the form presented, thousands of Americans made their first acquaintance with them.

Most of the facsimiles are from originals in the Huntington Library. Several have been lent by other institutions. In any event they represent the first or very early issues in pamphlet form. I am indebted to Mr. Carey S. Bliss, Miss Constance Lodge, and Mr. Erwin Morkisch of the Huntington Library for assistance in this undertaking.

J. E. P.

Huntington Library
San Marino, Calif.

GREAT AMERICANS SPEAK

BENJAMIN FRANKLIN

Benjamin Franklin

>·>·>·>·>·>·>·>·>·>·>·>·>·>·>·>·>·<·<·<·<·<·<·<·<·<·<·<·<·<·<·<·<·<

Examination by the House of Commons, 1766

THE STAMP ACT was passed by Parliament in March, 1765. Franklin, in London at the time, was amazed at its hostile reception in America. Petitions and remonstrances poured in from colonial assemblies, the Sons of Liberty was formed, and the Stamp Act Congress convened. And when the Act went into force in November, words were followed by deeds. America had friends in England; powerful individuals such as Pitt and Burke, but above all the British merchants who stood to lose by a boycott on British goods. On February 3, 1766, Franklin, who had been working for repeal, was summoned before the House of Commons, where, a few days later, with consummate skill he argued against the imposition of direct taxes by Parliament. No orator, Franklin had never appeared so long before so large an audience, nor was he ever to do so again. The Stamp Act was repealed a month later. Little attention was paid to the accompanying Declaratory Act which announced categorically that Parliament had the right to enact laws binding the colonies "in all cases whatsoever." Thus, though the American triumph was short-lived, America was on record.

Only the first twelve of fifty pages are reproduced here since, as in all such examinations, there is a good deal of repetition and reiteration. The *Examination* was printed in London, Boston, New York, Philadelphia, and New London in 1766. This is a facsimile of the first, or London, edition. The pamphlet was issued without a title page and the printer is unknown.

THE

EXAMINATION

O F

Doctor BENJAMIN FRANKLIN, &c.

Q. WHAT is your name, and place of abode?

A. Franklin, of Philadelphia.

Q. Do the Americans pay any considerable taxes among themselves?

A. Certainly many, and very heavy taxes.

Q. What are the present taxes in Pennsylvania, laid by the laws of the colony?

A. There are taxes on all estates real and personal, a poll tax, a tax on all offices, professions, trades and businesses, according to their profits; an excise on all wine, rum, and other spirits; and a duty of Ten Pounds per head on all Negroes imported, with some other duties.

Q. For what purposes are those taxes laid?

B   A. For

A. For the fupport of the civil and military eftablifhments of the country, and to difcharge the heavy debt contracted in the laft war.

Q. How long are thofe taxes to continue?

A. Thofe for difcharging the debt are to continue till 1772, and longer, if the debt fhould not be then all difcharged. The others muft always continue.

Q. Was it not expected that the debt would have been fooner difcharged?

A. It was, when the peace was made with France and Spain—But a frefh war breaking out with the Indians, a frefh load of debt was incurred, and the taxes, of courfe, continued longer by a new law.

Q. Are not all the people very able to pay thofe taxes?

A. No. The frontier counties, all along the continent, having been frequently ravaged by the enemy, and greatly impoverifhed, are able to pay very little tax. And therefore, in confideration of their diftreffes, our late tax laws do exprefsly favour thofe counties, excufing the fufferers; and I fuppofe the fame is done in other governments.

Q. Are not you concerned in the management of the Poft-Office in America?

A. Yes. I am Deputy Poft-Mafter General of North-America.

Q. Don't

Q. Don't you think the diftribution of ftamps, by poft, to all the inhabitants, very practicable, if there was no oppofition?

A. The pofts only go along the fea-coafts; they do not, except in a few inftances, go back into the country; and if they did, fending for ftamps by poft would occafion an expence of poftage, amounting, in many cafes, to much more than that of the ftamps themfelves.

Q. Are you acquainted with New-foundland?

A. I never was there.

Q. Do you know whether there are any poft-roads on that ifland?

A. I have heard that there are no roads at all; but that the communication between one fettlement and another is by fea only.

Q. Can you difperfe the ftamps by poft in Canada?

A. There is only a poft between Montreal and Quebec. The inhabitants live fo fcattered and remote from each other, in that vaft country, that pofts cannot be fupported among them, and therefore they cannot get ftamps per poft. The Englifh Colonies too, along the frontiers, are very thinly fettled.

B 2   Q. From

Q. From the thinness of the back set-tlements, would not the stamp-act be ex-tremely inconvenient to the inhabitants, if executed?

A. To be sure it would; as many of the inhabitants could not get stamps when they had occasion for them, without tak-ing long journeys, and spending perhaps Three or Four Pounds, that the Crown might get Sixpence.

Q. Are not the Colonies, from their circumstances, very able to pay the stamp duty.

A. In my opinion, there is not gold and silver enough in the Colonies to pay the stamp duty for one year.

Q. Don't you know that the money arising from the stamps was all to be laid out in America?

A. I know it is appropriated by the act to the American service; but it will be spent in the conquered Colonies, where the soldiers are, not in the Colonies that pay it.

Q. Is there not a balance of trade due from the Colonies where the troops are posted, that will bring back the money to the old colonies?

A. I think not. I believe very little would come back. I know of no trade likely to bring it back. I think it would come from the Colonies where it was

spent

ſpent directly to England; for I have always obſerved, that in every Colony the more plenty the means of remittance to England, the more goods are ſent for, and the more trade with England carried on.

Q. What number of white inhabitants do you think there are in Pennſylvania ?

A. I ſuppoſe there may be about 160,000.

Q. What number of them are Quakers?

A. Perhaps a third.

Q. What number of Germans?

A. Perhaps another third; but I cannot ſpeak with certainty.

Q. Have any number of the Germans ſeen ſervice, as ſoldiers, in Europe ?

A. Yes,—many of them, both in Europe and America.

Q. Are they as much diſſatisfied with the ſtamp-duty as the Engliſh ?

A. Yes, and more; and with reaſon, as their ſtamps are, in many caſes, to be double.

Q. How many white men do you ſuppoſe there are in North-America ?

A. About 300,000, from ſixteen to ſixty years of age.

Q. What may be the amount of one year's imports into Pennſylvania from Britain ?

A. I have been informed that our merchants

chants compute the imports from Britain to be above 500,000 Pounds.

Q. What may be the amount of the produce of your province exported to Britain?

A. It muſt be ſmall, as we produce little that is wanted in Britain. I ſuppoſe it cannot exceed 40,000 Pounds.

Q. How then do you pay the balance?

A. The balance is paid by our produce carried to the Weſt-Indies, and ſold in our own iſlands, or to the French, Spaniards, Danes and Dutch; by the ſame carried to other colonies in North-America, as to New-England, Nova-Scotia, Newfoundland, Carolina and Georgia; by the ſame carried to different parts of Europe, as Spain, Portugal and Italy. In all which places we receive either money, bills of Exchange, or commodities that ſuit for remittance to Britain; which, together with all the profits on the induſtry of our merchants and mariners, ariſing in thoſe circuitous voyages, and the freights made by their ſhips, center finally in Britain to diſcharge the balance, and pay for Britiſh manfactures continually uſed in the province, or ſold to foreigners by our traders.

Q. Have you heard of any difficulties lately laid on the Spaniſh trade?

A. Yes,

A. Yes, I have heard that it has been greatly obstructed by some new regulations, and by the English men of war and cutters stationed all along the coast in America.

Q. Do you think it right that America should be protected by this country, and pay no part of the expence?

A. That is not the case. The Colonies raised, cloathed and payed, during the last war, near 25000 men, and spent many millions.

Q. Were you not reimbursed by parliament?

A. We were only reimbursed what, in your opinion, we had advanced beyond our proportion, or beyond what might reasonably be expected from us; and it was a very small part of what we spent. Pennsylvania, in particular, disbursed about 500,000 Pounds, and the reimbursements, in the whole, did not exceed 60,000 Pounds.

Q. You have said that you pay heavy taxes in Pennsylvania; what do they amount to in the Pound?

A. The tax on all estates, real and personal, is Eighteen Pence in the Pound, fully rated; and the tax on the profits of trades and professions, with other taxes, do, I suppose, make full Half a Crown in the Pound.

Q. Do

Q. Do you know any thing of the rate of exchange in Pennſylvania, and whether it has fallen lately?

A. It is commonly from 170 to 175. I have heard that it has fallen lately from 175 to 162 and a half, owing, I ſuppoſe, to their leſſening their orders for goods; and when their debts to this country are paid, I think the exchange will probably be at par.

Q. Do not you think the people of America would ſubmit to pay the ſtamp-duty, if it was moderated?

A. No, never, unleſs compelled by force of arms.

Q. Are not the taxes in Pennſylvania laid on unequally, in order to burthen the Engliſh trade, particularly the tax on profeſſions and buſineſs?

A. It is not more burthenſome in pro-portion than the tax on lands. It is in-tended, and ſuppoſed to take an equal pro-portion of profits.

Q. How is the aſſembly compoſed? Of what kinds of people are the members, landholders or traders?

A. It is compoſed of landholders, mer-chants and artificers.

Q. Are not the majority landholders?

A. I believe they are.

Q. Do not they, as much as poſſible,
ſhift

shift the tax off from the land, to ease that, and lay the burthen heavier on trade?

A. I have never understood it so. I never heard such a thing suggested. And indeed an attempt of that kind could answer no purpose. The merchant or trader is always skilled in figures, and ready with his pen and ink. If unequal burthens are laid on his trade, he puts an additional price on his goods; and the consumers, who are chiefly landholders, finally pay the greatest part, if not the whole.

Q. What was the temper of America towards Great-Britain before the year 1763?

A. The best in the world. They submitted willingly to the government of the Crown, and paid, in all their courts, obedience to acts of parliament. Numerous as the people are in the several old provinces, they cost you nothing in forts, citadels, garrisons or armies, to keep them in subjection. They were governed by this country at the expence only of a little pen, ink and paper. They were led by a thread. They had not only a respect, but an affection, for Great-Britain, for its laws, its customs and manners, and even a fondness for its fashions, that greatly increased the commerce. Natives

C   of

of Britain were always treated with particular regard; to be an Old England-man was, of itself, a character of some respect, and gave a kind of rank among us.

Q. And what is their temper now.

A. O, very much altered.

Q. Did you ever hear the authority of parliament to make laws for America questioned till lately?

A. The authority of parliament was allowed to be valid in all laws, except such as should lay internal taxes. It was never disputed in laying duties to regulate commerce.

Q. In what proportion hath population increased in America?

A. I think the inhabitants of all the provinces together, taken at a medium, double in about 25 years. But their demand for British manufactures increases much faster, as the consumption is not merely in proportion to their numbers, but grows with the growing abilities of the same numbers to pay for them. In 1723, the whole importation from Britain to Pennsylvania, was but about 15,000 Pounds Sterling; it is now near Half a Million.

Q. In what light did the people of America use to consider the parliament of Great-Britain?

A. They

A. They confidered the parliament as the great bulwark and fecurity of their liberties and privileges, and always fpoke of it with the utmoft refpect and veneration. Arbitrary minifters, they thought, might poffibly, at times, attempt to opprefs them; but they relied on it, that the parliament, on application, would always give redrefs. They remembered, with gratitude, a ftrong inftance of this, when a bill was brought into parliament, with a claufe, to make royal inftructions laws in the Colonies, which the Houfe of Commons would not pafs, and it was thrown out.

Q. And have they not ftill the fame refpect for parliament?

A. No; it is greatly leffened.

Q. To what caufes is that owing?

A. To a concurrence of caufes; the reftraints lately laid on their trade, by which the bringing of foreign gold and filver into the Colonies was prevented; the prohibition of making paper money among themfelves; and then demanding a new and heavy tax by ftamps; taking away, at the fame time, trials by juries, and refufing to receive and hear their humble petitions.

Q. Don't you think they would fubmit to the ftamp-act, if it was modified, the

C 2 obnoxious

obnoxious parts taken out, and the duty reduced to ſome particulars, of ſmall mo-ment ?

A. No; they will never ſubmit to it.

THOMAS PAINE

Thomas Paine

The American Crisis, 1776

TOWARD THE CLOSE OF 1776 the American cause was faltering badly. In December the army under General Washington —aide-de-camp Tom Paine with it—was beating a retreat through New Jersey. Morale was low, soldiers were deserting, and the Tory element was reasserting itself. It was at this juncture that the famous author of *Common Sense* wrote *The Crisis*, a ringing appeal in behalf of the Revolution. Once again Paine proved his genius for communicating and interpreting a great idea to men in all walks of life. When printed, *The Crisis* was said to have been read in camp to every corporal's guard. Although *The Crisis* did not win any battles, it certainly infused new vigor into a disheartened army. Moreover, at a crucial time it stiffened morale throughout the colonies. During the course of the War, Paine was to write other stirring numbers of *The Crisis*, but none so timely and electrifying as *No. 1*.

The American Crisis No. 1 was printed in the *Pennsylvania Journal* of December 19, 1776, under the pseudonym "Common Sense" and appeared in pamphlet form on December 23. This is a facsimile of one of the earliest separate printings. Since the Huntington Library copy contains several poorly printed pages, the Historical Society of Pennsylvania generously made its copy [printed by Melchior Steiner and Charles Cist, Philadelphia, 1776] available.

The *American* CRISIS.

NUMBER I.

By the Author of COMMON SENSE.

THESE are the times that try men's souls: The summer soldier and the sunshine patriot will, in this crisis, shrink from the service of his country; but he that stands it NOW, deserves the love and thanks of man and woman. Tyranny, like hell, is not easily conquered; yet we have this consolation with us, that the harder the conflict, the more glorious the triumph. What we obtain too cheap, we esteem too lightly:---'Tis dearness only that gives every thing its value. Heaven knows how to set a proper price upon its goods; and it would be strange indeed, if so celestial an article as FREEDOM should not be highly rated. Britain, with an army to enforce her tyranny, has declared, that she has a right *(not only to* TAX) but "*to* "BIND us *in* ALL CASES WHATSOEVER," and if being *bound in that manner* is not slavery, then is there not such a thing as slavery upon earth. Even the expression is impious, for so unlimited a power can belong only to GOD.

WHETHER the Independence of the Continent was declared too soon, or delayed too long, I will not now enter into as an argument; my own simple opinion is, that had it been eight months earlier, it would have been much better. We did not make a proper use of last winter, neither could we, while we were in a dependent state. However, the fault, if it were one, was all our own; we have none to blame but ourselves*. But no great deal is lost yet; all that Howe has been doing for this month past is rather a ravage than a conquest, which the spirit of the Jersies a year ago would have quickly repulsed, and which time and a little resolution will soon recover.

I have as little superstition in me as any man living, but my

---

* "The present winter" (meaning the last) "is worth an "age, if rightly employed, but if lost, or neglected, the whole "Continent will partake of the evil; and there is no punish- "ment that man does not deserve, be he who, or what, or "where he will, that may be the means of sacrificing a season "so precious and useful."　COMMON SENSE.

my fecret opinion has ever been, and ftill is, that GOD almighty will not give up a people to military deftruction, or leave them unfupportedly to perifh, who had fo earneftly and fo repeatedly fought to avoid the calamities of war, by every decent method which wifdom could invent. Neither have I fo much of the infidel in me, as to fuppofe, that HE has relinquifhed the government of the world, and given us up to the care of devils; and as I do not, I cannot fee on what grounds the king of Britain can look up to heaven for help againft us: A common murderer, a highwayman, or a houfebreaker, has as good a pretence as he.

'TIS furprifing to fee how rapidly a panic will fometimes run through a country. All nations and ages have been fubject to them: Britain has trembled like an ague at the report of a French fleet of flat bottomed boats; and in the fourteenth century the whole Englifh army, after ravaging the kingdom of France, was driven back like men pe-trified with fear; and this brave exploit was performed by a few broken forces collected and headed by a woman, Joan of Arc. Would, that Heaven might infpire fome Jerfey maid to fpirit up her countrymen, and fave her fair fellow-fufferers from ravage and ravifhment! Yet panics, in fome cafes, have their ufes; they produce as much good as hurt. Their duration is always fhort; the mind foon grows thro' them, and acquires a firmer habit than before. But their pe-culiar advantage is, that they are the touchftones of fincerity and hypocrify, and bring things and men to light, which might otherwife have lain for ever undifcovered. In fact, they have the fame effect on fecret traitors, which an ima-ginary apparition would upon a private murderer. They fift out the hidden thoughts of man, and hold them up in public to the world. Many a difguifed Tory has lately fhewn his head, that fhall penitentially folemnize with curfes the day on which Howe arrived upon the Delaware.

As I was with the troops at fort Lee, and marched with them to the edge of Pennfylvania, I am well acquainted with many circumftances, which thofe, who lived at a diftance, know but little or nothing of. Our fituation there was ex-ceedingly cramped, the place being on a narrow neck of land between the North river and the Hackenfack. Our force was inconfiderable, being not one fourth fo great as Howe could bring againft us. We had no army at hand to
have

have relieved the garrifon, had we fhut ourfelves up and
ftood on the defence. Our ammunition, light artillery, and
the beft part of our ftores, had been removed upon the apprehenfion that Howe would endeavour to penetrate the
Jerfies, in which cafe fort Lee could be of no ufe to us;
for it muft occur to every thinking man, whether in the
army or not, that thefe kind of field forts are only for temporary purpofes, and laft in ufe no longer than the enemy
directs his force againft the particular object, which fuch forts
are raifed to defend. Such was our fituation and condition
at fort Lee on the morning of the 20th of November, when
an officer arrived with information, that the enemy with
200 boats had landed about feven or eight miles above :
Major General Green, who commanded the garrifon, immediately ordered them under arms, and fent exprefs to his
Excellency General Wafhington at the town of Hackenfack, diftant by the way of the ferry fix miles. Our firft
object was to fecure the bridge over the Hackenfack, which
laid up the river between the enemy and us, about fix miles
from us and three from them. General Wafhington arrived
in about three quarters of an hour, and marched at the head
of the troops towards the bridge, which place I expected we
fhould have a brufh for; however they did not chufe to
difpute it with us, and the greateft part of our troops went
over the bridge, the reft over the ferry, except fome which
paffed at a mill on a fmall creek, between the bridge and
the ferry, and made their way through fome marfhy grounds
up to the town of Hackenfack, and there paffed tne river.
We brought off as much baggage as the waggons could
contain, the reft was loft. The fimple object was to bring
off the garrifon, and to march them on till they could be
ftrengthened by the Jerfey or Pennfylvania militia, fo as to
be enabled to make a ftand. We ftaid four days at Newark,
collected in our out-pofts with fome of the Jerfey militia,
and marched out twice to meet the enemy on information
of their being advancing, though our numbers were greatly
inferiour to theirs. Howe, in my little opinion, committed
a great error in generalfhip, in not throwing a body of
forces off from Staaten Ifland through Amboy, by which
means he might have feized all our ftores at Brunfwick, and
intercepted our march into Pennfylvania : But, if we believe the power of hell to be limited, we muft likewife believe

lieve that their agents are under some providential controul.

I shall not now attempt to give all the particulars of our retreat to the Delaware; suffice it for the present to say, that both officers and men, though greatly harassed and fatigued, frequently without rest, covering, or provision, the inevitable consequences of a long retreat, bore it with a manly and a martial spirit. All their wishes were one, which was, that the country would turn out and help them to drive the enemy back. Voltaire has remarked, that king William never appeared to full advantage but in difficulties and in action; the same remark may be made on General Washington, for the character fits him. There is a natural firmness in some minds which cannot be unlocked by triffles, but which, when unlocked, discovers a cabinet of fortitude; and I reckon it among those kind of public blessings, which we do not immediately see, that GOD hath blest him with uninterrupted health, and given him a mind that can even flourish upon care.

I shall conclude this paper with some miscellaneous remarks on the state of our affairs; and shall begin with asking the following question, Why is it that the enemy hath left the New-England provinces, and made these middle ones the seat of war? The answer is easy: New-England is not infested with Tories, and we are. I have been tender in raising the cry against these men, and used numberless arguments to shew them their danger, but it will not do to sacrifice a world to either their folly or their baseness. The period is now arrived, in which either they or we must change our sentiments, or one or both must fall. And what is a Tory? Good GOD! what is he? I should not be afraid to go with an hundred Whigs against a thousand Tories, were they to attempt to get into arms. Every Tory is a coward, for a servile, slavish, self-interested fear is the foundation of Toryism; and a man under such influence, though he may be cruel, never can be brave.

BUT before the line of irrecoverable seperation be drawn between us, let us reason the matter together: Your conduct is an invitation to the enemy, yet not one in a thousand of you has heart enough to join him. Howe is as much deceived by you as the American cause is injured by you. He expects you will all take up arms, and flock to his standard with muskets on your shoulders. Your opinions
are

are of no use to him, unless you support him personally; for 'tis soldiers, and not Tories, that he wants.

I once felt all that kind of anger, which a man ought to feel, against the mean principles that are held by the Tories: A noted one, who kept a tavern at Amboy, was standing at his door, with as pretty a child in his hand, about eight or nine years old, as most I ever saw, and after speaking his mind as freely as he thought was prudent, finished with this unfatherly expression, "*Well! give me peace in my day.*" Not a man lives on the Continent but fully believes that a seperation must some time or other finally take place, and a generous parent would have said, "*If there must be trouble, let it be in my day, that my child may have peace;*" and this single reflection, well applied, is sufficient to awaken every man to duty. Not a place upon earth might be so happy as America. Her situation is remote from all the wrangling world, and she has nothing to do but to trade with them. A man may easily distinguish in himself between temper and principle, and I am as confident, as I am that GOD governs the world, that America will never be happy till she gets clear of foreign dominion. Wars, without ceasing, will break out till that period arrives, and the Continent must in the end be conqueror; for, though the flame of liberty may sometimes cease to shine, the coal never can expire.

AMERICA did not, nor does not, want force; but she wanted a proper application of that force. Wisdom is not the purchase of a day, and it is no wonder that we should err at first sitting off. From an excess of tenderness, we were unwilling to raise an army, and trusted our cause to the temporary defence of a well meaning militia. A summer's experience has now taught us better; yet with those troops, while they were collected, we were able to set bounds to the progress of the enemy, and, thank GOD! they are again assembling. I always considered a militia as the best troops in the world for a sudden exertion, but they will not do for a long campaign. Howe, it is probable, will make an attempt on this city; should he fail on this side the Delaware, he is ruined; if he succeeds, our cause is not ruined. He stakes all on his side against a part on ours; admitting he succeeds, the consequence will be, that armies from both ends of the Continent will march to assist their

suffer-

suffering friends in the middle States; for he cannot go every where, it is impossible. I consider Howe as the greatest enemy the Tories have; he is bringing a war into their country, which, had it not been for him and partly for themselves, they had been clear of. Should he now be expelled, I wish, with all the devotion of a Christian, that the names of Whig and Tory may never more be mentioned; but should the Tories give him encouragement to come, or assistance if he come, I as sincerely wish that our next year's arms may expell them from the Continent, and the Congress appropriate their possessions to the relief of those who have suffered in well doing. A single successful battle next year will settle the whole. America could carry on a two years war by the confiscation of the property of disaffected persons, and be made happy by their expulsion. Say not that this is revenge, call it rather the soft resentment of a suffering people, who, having no object in view but the GOOD OF ALL, have staked their OWN ALL upon a seemingly doubtful event. Yet it is folly to argue against determined hardness; eloquence may strike the ear, and the language of sorrow draw forth the tear of compassion, but nothing can reach the heart that is steeled with prejudice.

QUITTING this class of men, I turn with the warm ardour of a friend to those who have nobly stood, and are yet determined to stand the matter out: I call not upon a few, but upon all; not on THIS State or THAT State, but on EVERY State; up and help us; lay your shoulders to the wheel; better have too much force than too little, when so great an object is at stake. Let it be told to the future world, that in the depth of winter, when nothing but hope and virtue could survive, that the city and the country, alarmed at one common danger, came forth to meet and to repulse it. Say not, that thousands are gone, turn out your tens of thousands; throw not the burthen of the day upon Providence, but " *shew your faith by your works,*" that GOD may bless you. It matters not where you live, or what rank of life you hold, the evil or the blessing will reach you all. The far and the near, the home counties and the back, the rich and the poor, shall suffer or rejoice alike. The heart that feels not now, is dead: The blood of his children shall curse his cowardice, who shrinks back at a time when a little might have saved the whole, and made *them* happy. I love
the

the man that can smile in trouble, that can gather strength from distress, and grow brave by reflection. 'Tis the business of little minds to shrink; but he whose heart is firm, and whose conscience approves his conduct, will pursue his principles unto death. My own line of reasoning is to myself as strait and clear as a ray of light. Not all the treasures of the world, so far as I believe, could have induced me to support an offensive war, for I think it murder; but if a thief break into my house, burn and destroy my property, and kill or threaten to kill me, or those that are in it, and to " *bind me in all cases whatsoever*," to his absolute will, am I to suffer it? What signifies it to me, whether he who does it, is a king or a common man; my countryman or not my countryman? whether it is done by an individual villain, or an army of them? If we reason to the root of things we shall find no difference; neither can any just cause be assigned why we should punish in the one case, and pardon in the other. Let them call me rebel, and welcome, I feel no concern from it; but I should suffer the misery of devils, were I to make a whore of my soul by swearing allegiance to one, whose character is that of a sottish, stuped, stubborn, worthless, brutish man. I conceive likewise a horrid idea in receiving mercy from a being, who at the last day shall be shrieking to the rocks and mountains to cover him, and fleeing with terror from the orphan, the widow and the slain of America.

THERE are cases which cannot be overdone by language, and this is one. There are persons too who see not the full extent of the evil that threatens them; they solace themselves with hopes that the enemy, if they succeed, will be merciful. It is the madness of folly to expect mercy from those who have refused to do justice; and even mercy, where conquest is the object, is only a trick of war: The cunning of the fox is as murderous as the violence of the wolfe; and we ought to guard equally against both. Howe's first object is partly by threats and partly by promises, to terrify or seduce the people to deliver up their arms, and receive mercy. The ministry recommended the same plan to Gage, and this is what the Tories call making their peace; " *a peace which passeth all understanding*" indeed! A peace which would be the immediate forerunner of a worse ruin than any we have yet thought of. Ye men of Pennsylvania, do reason upon those things! Were the back counties

ties to give up their arms, they would fall an eafy prey to the Indians, who are all armed : This perhaps is what fome Tories would not be forry for. Were the home counties to deliver up their arms, they would be expofed to the refentment of the back counties, who would then have it in their power to chaftife their defection at pleafure. And were any one State to give up its arms, THAT State muft be garrifoned by all Howe's army of Britons and Heffians to preferve it from the anger of the reft. Mutual fear is a principal link in the chain of mutual love, and woe be to that State that breaks the compact. Howe is mercifully inviting you to barbarous deftruction, and men muft be either rogues or fools that will not fee it. I dwell not upon the vapours of imagination; I bring reafon to your ears ; and in language, as plain as A, B, C, hold up truth to your eyes.

I thank GOD that I fear not. I fee no real caufe for fear. I know our fituation well, and can fee the way out of it. While our army was collected Howe dared not rifk a battle, and it is no credit to him that he decamped from the White Plains, and waited a mean opportunity to ravage the defencelefs Jerfies ; but it is great credit to us, that, with an handful of men, we fuftained an orderly retreat for near an hundred miles, brought off our ammunition, all our fieldpieces, the greateft part of our ftores, and had four rivers to pafs. None can fay that our retreat was precipitate, for we were near three weeks in performing it, that the country might have time to come in. Twice we marched back to meet the enemy and remained out till dark. The fign of fear was not feen in our camp, and had not fome of the cowardly and difaffected inhabitants fpread falfe alarms thro' the country, the Jerfies had never been ravaged. Once more we are again collected and collecting ; our new army at both ends of the Continent is recruiting faft, and we fhall be able to open the next campaign with fixty thoufand men, well armed and cloathed. This is our fituation, and who will may know it. By perfeverance and fortitude we have the profpect of a glorious iffue ; by cowardice and fubmiffion, the fad choice of a variety of evils---a ravaged country---a depopulated city---habitations without fafety, and flavery without hope---our homes turned into barracks and baudy-houfes for Heffians, and a future race to provide for whofe fathers we fhall doubt of. Look on this picture, and weep over it !---and if there yet remains one thoughtlefs wretch who believes it not, let him fuffer it unlamented.

GEORGE WASHINGTON

George Washington

※※※※※※※※※※※※※※※※※※※※≪≪≪≪≪≪≪≪≪≪≪≪≪≪≪≪

Farewell Address, 1796

IN SEPTEMBER, 1796, President Washington delivered one of the great presidential addresses. It is marked by wisdom and clarity, and a sincere eloquence. In the most gracious of words he explained why he felt it unwise to seek a third term. Then, as one who had devoted his whole adult life to the service of his country, he ventured to offer the young Republic advice and guidance. This address is remembered by most for its warning against foreign involvements, especially entangling alliances. Overlooked, however, are Washington's views upon a strong union; that the central government should serve all sections, the North and the South, the East and the great new West. More pungent were his admonitions on party and faction. It was his opinion that the spirit of party recently manifested, must never be permitted to transcend devotion to the government. Political parties controlled by calculating and cunning men, he warned, might subvert good government and ultimately destroy the liberties of the people. In Washington's measured and seasoned utterances one finds astonishing freshness and timeliness.

The Farewell Address was first published in the *Daily Advertiser* of New York on September 17, 1796. This is a facsimile of the first separate printing, published in the same year at Philadelphia.

THE PRESIDENT'S

Addreſs to the People of the

United States.

FRIENDS, AND FELLOW-CITIZENS,

THE period for a new election of a Citizen, to administer the executive government of the United States, being not far diſtant, and the time actually arrived, when your thoughts muſt be employed in deſignating the perſon, who is to be cloathed with that important truſt, it appears to me proper, eſpecially as it may conduce to a more diſtinct expreſſion of the public voice, that I ſhould now appriſe you of the reſolution I have formed, to decline being conſidered among the number of thoſe, out of whom a choice is to be made.

I BEG you, at the ſame time, to do me the juſtice to be aſſured, that this reſolution has not been taken, without a ſtrict regard to all the conſiderations appertaining to the relation, which binds a dutiful citizen to his country ; and that, in withdrawing the tender of ſervice which ſilence in my ſituation might imply, I am influenced by no diminution of zeal for your future intereſt ; no deficiency of grateful reſpect for your paſt kindneſs : but am ſupported by a full conviction that the ſtep is compatible with both.

THE acceptance of, and continuance hitherto in the office to which your ſuffrages have twice called me, have been a uniform ſacrifice of inclination to the opinion of duty, and to a deference for what appeared to be your deſire. I conſtantly hoped, that it would have been much earlier in my power, conſiſtently with motives, which I was not at liberty to diſregard, to return to that retirement, from which I had been reluctantly drawn. The ſtrength of my inclination to do this, previous to the laſt election, had even led to that

the preparation of an addrefs to declare it to you ; but mature reflection on the then perplexed and critical pofture of
our affairs with foreign nations, and the unanimous advice
of perfons entitled to my confidence, impelled me to abandon the idea.

I REJOICE, that the ftate of your concerns, external as
well as internal, no longer renders the purfuit of inclination
incompatible with the fentiment of duty, or propriety : and
am perfuaded whatever partiality may be retained for my
fervice, that in the prefent circumftances of our country,
you will not difapprove of my determination to retire.

THE impreffions with which I firft undertook the ardu-
ous truft, were explained on the proper occafion.   In the
difcharge of this truft, I will only fay, that I have with good
intentions, contributed towards the organization and adminiftration of the government, the beft exertions of which a
very fallible judgment was capable.   Not unconfcious, in
the out-fet, of the inferiority of my qualifications, experience in my own eyes, perhaps, ftill more in the eyes of o-
thers, has ftrengthened the motives to diffidence of myfelf :
and every day the encreafing weight of years admonifhes me
more and more, that the fhade of retirement is as neceffary
to me as it will be welcome.   Satisfied that if any circumftances have given peculiar value to my fervices, they were
temporary, I have the confolation to believe, that while
choice and prudence invite me to quit the political fcene,
patriotifm does not forbid it.

IN looking forward to the moment, which is intended
to terminate the career of my public life, my feelings do
not permit me to fufpend the deep acknowledgment of that
debt of gratitude which I owe to my beloved country, for
the many honors it has conferred upon me ; ftill more for
the ftedfaft confidence with which it has fupported me ; and
for the opportunities I have thence enjoyed of manifefting
my inviolable attachment, by fervices faithful and perfever-
ing, though in ufefulnefs unequal to my zeal.   If benefits
have refulted to our country from thefe fervices, let it always be remembered to our praife, and as an inftructive example in our annals, that under circumftances in which the
paffions, agitated in every direction, were liable to miflead,

amidft

amidst appearances sometimes dubious—viciffitudes of fortune often difcouraging—in fituations in which not unfrequently want of fuccefs has countenanced the fpirit of criticifm—the conftancy of your support was the effential prop of the efforts, and a guarantee of the plans by which they were effected—Profoundly penetrated with this idea, I fhall carry it with me to my grave, as a ftrong incitement to unceafing vows that Heaven may continue to you the choiceft tokens of its beneficence—that your union and brotherly affection may be perpetual—that the free conftitution, which is the work of your hands, may be facredly maintained—that its adminiftration in every department may be ftamped with wifdom and virtue—that, in fine, the happinefs of the people of thefe States, under the aufpices of liberty, may be made complete, by fo careful a prefervation and fo prudent a ufe of this bleffing, as will acquire to them the glory of recommending it to the applaufe, the affection and adoption of every nation which is yet a ftranger to it.

HERE, perhaps, I ought to ftop. But a folicitude for your welfare, which cannot end but with my life, and the apprehenfion of danger natural to that folicitude, urge me on an occafion like the prefent, to offer to your folemn contemplation, and to recommend to your frequent review, fome fentiments, which are the refult of much reflection, of no inconfiderable obfervation, and which appear to me all-important to the permanency of your felicity as a people. Thefe will be offered to you with the more freedom, as you can only feel in them the difinterefted warnings of a parting friend, who can poffibly have no perfonal motive to bias his counfels. Nor can I forget, as an encouragement to it, your indulgent reception of my fentiments on a former and not diffimilar occafion.

INTERWOVEN as is the love of liberty with every ligament of your hearts, no recommendation of mine is neceffary to fortify or confirm the attachment.

THE unity of government which conftitute you one people, is alfo dear to you. It is juftly fo; for it is a main pillar in the edifice of your real independence, the fupport of your tranquility at home, your peace abroad ;——— of your fafety ;———of your profperity ; — of that very

liberty

liberty which you fo highly prize.   But, as it is eafy to
forefee, that from different caufes and from different quarters, much pains will be taken, many artifices employed, to
weaken in your minds the conviction of this truth ; as this
is the point in your political fortrefs againft which the bat-
teries of internal and external enemies will be moft conftantly and actively (though often covertly and infiduoufly)
directed, it is of infinite moment, that you fhould properly
eftimate the immenfe value of your national Union, to your
collective and individual happinefs; that you fhould cherifh
a cordial, habitual and immoveable attachment to it : ac-
cuftoming yourfelves to think and fpeak of it as of the pal-
ladium of your political fafety and profperity ; watching for
its prefervation with jealous anxiety ; difcountenancing
whatever may fuggeft even a fufpicion that it can in any e-
vent be abandoned ; and indignantly frowning upon the
firft dawning of every attempt to alienate any portion of our
country from the reft, or to enfeeble the facred ties which
now link together the various parts.

FOR this you have every inducement of fympathy and
intereft.   Citizens by birth or choice, of a common country,
that country has a right to countenance your affections.
The name AMERICAN, which belongs to you, in your
national capacity, muft always exalt the juft pride of patriotifm, more than any appellation derived from local difcri-
mination.   With flight fhades of difference, you have the
fame religion, manners, habits and political principles ——
You have, in a common caufe, fought and triumphed together ; the independence and liberty you poffefs are the work
of joint councils, and joint efforts, of common dangers, fuf-
ferings and fuccefes.

BUT thefe confiderations, however powerfully they addrefs themfelves to your fenfibility, are greatly outweighed
by thofe which apply more immediately to your intereft.
Here every portion of our country finds the moft com-
manding motives for carefully guarding and preferving the
Union of the whole.

THE *North*, in an unreftrained intercourfe with the
South, protected by the equal laws of a common government, finds in the productions of the latter, great additional
resources

resources of maritime and commercial enterprise, and precious materials of manufacturing industry. The *South*, in the same intercourse, benefitting by the agency of the *North*, sees its agriculture grow and its commerce expand. Turning partly into its own channels the seamen of the North, it finds its particular navigation invigorated—and while it contributes, in different ways, to nourish and increase the general mass of the national navigation, it looks forward to the protection of a maritime strength, to which itself is unequally adapted. The *East* in a like intercourse with the *West*, already finds, and in the progressive improvement of interior communications, by land and water, will more and more find a valuable vent for the commodities which it brings from abroad, or manufactures at home. The *West* derives from the *East* supplies requisite to its growth and comfort—and what is perhaps of still greater consequence, it must of necessity owe the *secure* enjoyment of indispensable *outlets* for its own productions to the weight, influence, and the future maritime strength of the Atlantic side of the Union, directed by an indissoluble community of interest as *one nation*. Any other tenure by which the *West* can hold this essential advantage, whether derived from its own separate strength, or from an apostate and unnatural connection with any foreign power, must be intrinsically precarious.

WHILE then every part of our country thus feels an immediate and particular interest in Union, all the parts combined cannot fail to find in the united mass of means and efforts greater strength, greater resource, proportionably greater security from external danger, a less frequent interruption of their peace by foreign nations ; and what is of most inestimable value ! they must derive from Union an exemption from those broils and wars between themselves, which so frequently afflict neighboring countries, not tied together by the same government ; which their own rivalships alone would be sufficient to produce, but which opposite foreign alliances, attachments and intrigues would stimulate and imbitter. Hence likewise they will avoid the necessity of those overgrown military establishments, which under any form of government are inauspicious fpicious to liberty, and which are to be regarded as particularly hoftile to Republican Liberty: In this fenfe it is, that your Union ought to be confidered as a main prop of your liberty, and that the love of the one ought to endear to you the prefervation of the other.

THESE confiderations fpeak a perfuafive language to every reflecting and virtuous mind, and exhibit the continuance of the UNION as a primary object of patriotic defire. Is there a doubt, whether a common government can embrace fo large a fphere ?—Let experience folve it. To liften to mere fpeculation in fuch a cafe were criminal. We are authorifed to hope that a proper organization of the whole, with the auxiliary agency of governments for the refpective fubdivifions, will afford a happy iffue to the experiment. 'Tis well worth a fair and full experiment. With fuch powerful and obvious motives to Union, effecting all parts of our country, while experiment fhall not have demonftrated its impracticability, there will always be reafon to diftruft the patriotifm of thofe, who in any quarter may endeavour to weaken its bands.

IN contemplating the caufes which may difturb our Union it occurs as matter of ferious concern, that any ground fhould have been furnifhed for characterifing parties by *Geographical* difcriminations—*Northern* and *Southern*—*Atlantic* and *Weftern* ; whence defigning men may endeavour to excite a belief that there is a real difference of local interefts and views. One of thefe expedients of party to acquire influence, within particular diftricts, is to mifreprefent the opinions and aims of other diftricts. You cannot fhield yourfelves too much againft the jealoufies and heart burnings which fpring from thofe mifreprefentations ; they tend to render alien to each other thofe who ought to be bound together by fraternal affection. The inhabitants of our weftern country have lately had a ufeful leffon on this head : they have feen, in the negociation by the Executive, and in the unanimous ratification by the Senate, of the treaty with Spain, and in the univerfal fatisfaction at that event, throughout the United States, a decifive proof how unfounded were the fufpicions propagated among them of a policy in the general government and in the Atlantic States unfriendly to

their

their interefts in regard to the MISSISIPPI : they have been
witneffes to the formation of two treaties, that with Great-
Britain and that with Spain, which fecure to them every
thing they could defire, in refpect to our foreign relations,
towards confirming their profperity. Will it not be their
wifdom to rely for their prefervation of thefe advantages on
the UNION by which they were procured ? Will they not
henceforth be deaf to thofe advifers, if fuch there are, who
would fever them from their Brethren and connect them with
aliens ?

To the efficacy and permenency of your Union, a Government for the whole is indifpenfable—No alliences, however ftrict, between the parts can be an adequate fubftitute;
they muft inevitably experience the infractions and inter-
ruptions which all alliances in all times have experienced.
Senfible of this momentous truth, you have improved upon
your firft effay, by the adoption of a Conftitution of Government better calculated than your former for an intimite
Union, and for the efficacious management of your common
concerns. This Government, the offspring of our own
choice, uninfluenced and unawed, adopted upon full invef-
tigation and mature deliberation, completely free in its principles, in the diftribution of its powers, uniting fecurity with
energy, and containing within itfelf a provifion for its own
amendment, has a juft claim to your confidence and your
fupport. Refpect for its authority, compliance with its
laws, acquiefcence in its meafures, are duties enjoined by
the fundamental maxims of true Liberty. The bafis of our
political fyftems is the right of the people to make and to
alter their Conftitution of government—But, the conftitution which at any time exifts, 'till changed by an explicit
and authentic act of the whole people, is facredly obligatory upon all. The very idea of the power and the right of
the people to eftablifh Government prefuppofes the duty of
every individual to obey the eftablifhed Government.

All obftructions to the execution of the Laws, all combinations and affociations, under whatever plaufible character, with the real defign to direct, controul, counteract, or
awe the regular deliberation and action of the conftituted
authorities, are deftructive of this fundamental principle,
and

and of fatal tendency. They ferve to organize faction, to give it an artificial and extraordinary force—to put in the place of the delegated will of the nation, the will of a party, often a fmall but artful and enterprifing minority of the community; and, according to the alternate triumphs of different parties, to make the public adminiftration the mirror of the ill conceited and incongruous projects of faction, rather than the organ of confiftent and wholefome plans digefted by common councils, and modified by mutual interefts.

However combinations or affociations of the above defcription, may now and then anfwer popular ends, they are likely in the courfe of time and things, to become potent engines, by which cunning, ambitious and unprincipled men, will be enabled to fubvert the power of the people, and to ufurp for themfelves the reigns of government; deftroying afterwards the very engines which have lifted them to unjuft dominion.

Towards the prefervation of your government, and the permanency of your prefent happy ftate, it is requifite, not only that you fteadily difcountenance irregular oppofitions to its acknowledged authority, but alfo that you refift with care, the fpirit of innovation upon its principles, however fpecious the pretexts. One method of affault may be to effect in the forms of the conftitution, alterations which will impair the energy of the fyftem, and thus to undermine what cannot be directly overthrown. In all the changes to which you may be invited, remember that time and habit are at leaft as neceffary to fix the true character of government, as of other human inftitutions that experience is the fureft ftandard, by which to teft the real tendency of the exifting conftitution of a country—that facility in changes upon the credit of mere hypothefis and opinion, expofes to perpetual change, from the endlefs variety of hypothefis and opinion; and remember, efpecially, that for the efficient management of your common interefts, in a country fo extenfive as ours, a government of as much vigor as is confiftent with the perfect fecurity of liberty, is indifpenfible. Liberty itfelf will find in fuch a government, with powers properly diftributed and adjufted, its fureft guardian. It

is.

is, indeed, little elfe than a name, where the government is too feeble to withftand the enterprifes of faction, to confine each member of the fociety within the limits prefcribed by the laws, and to maintain all in the fecure and tranquil enjoyment of the rights of perfon and property.

I HAVE already intimated to you, the danger of parties in the ftate, with peculiar reference to the founding of them on geographical difcriminations. Let me now take a more comprehenfive view, and warn you in the moft folemn manner, againft the baneful effects of the fpirit of party, generally.

THIS fpirit, unfortunately, is infeperable from our nature, having its root in the ftrongeft paffions of the human mind. It exifts under different fhapes in all governments, more or lefs ftifled, controuled, or repreffed :—But in thofe of the popular form, it is feen in its greateft ranknefs, and is truly their worft enemy.

THE alternate domination of one faction over another, fharpened by the fpirit of revenge, natural to party diffention, which in different ages and countries has perpetrated the moft horrid enormities, is itfelf a frightful defpotifm— But this leads at length to a more formal and permanent defpotifm. The diforders and miferies, which refult, gradually incline the minds of men to feek fecurity, and repofe in the abfolute power of an individual ; and fooner or later the chief of fome prevailing faction more able or more fortunate than his competitors, turns this difpofition to the purpofes of his own elevation, on the ruins of public liberty.

WITHOUT looking forward to an extremity of this kind (which, neverthelefs, ought not to be entirely out of fight) the common and continual mifchiefs of the fpirit of party, are fufficient to make it the intereft and duty of a wife people to difcourage and reftrain it.

IT ferves always to diftract the public councils, and enfeeble the public adminiftration. It agitates the community with ill founded jealoufies and falfe alarms ; kindles the animofity of one part againft another, foments occafionally riot and infurrection. It opens the door to foreign influence and corruption, which find a facilitated accefs to the government itfelf through the channels of party paffion.— Thus the policy and the will of one country are fubjected to the policy and will of another.   B

THERE is an opinion that parties in free countries are useful checks upon the administration of the government, and serve to keep alive the spirit of liberty. This within certain limits is probably true, and in governments of a monarchical cast, patriotism may look with indulgence, if not with favor upon the spirit of party. But in those of the popular character, in governments purely elective, it is a spirit not to be encouraged. From their natural tendency it is certain there will always be enough of that spirit for every salutary purpose. And there being constant danger of excess, the effort ought to be, by force of public opinion, to mitigate and assuage it. A fire not to be quenched; it demands uniform vigilance to prevent its bursting into a flame, lest instead of warming, it should consume.

IT is important likewise, that the habits of thinking in a free country, should inspire caution, in those entrusted with its administration, to confine themselves within their respective constitutional spheres, avoiding in the exercise of the powers of one department to encroach upon another. The spirit of encroachment tends to consolidate the powers of all departments in one, and thus to create, whatever the form of government, a real despotism. A just estimate of that love of power, and proneneness to abuse it, which predominates in the human heart, is sufficient to satisfy us of the truth of this position. The necessity of reciprocal checks in the exercise of the political power; by dividing and distributing it into different depositories, and constituting each the guardian of the public weal against invasions by the others, has been evinced by experiments ancient and modern : some of them in our country and under our own eyes. To preserve them must be as necessary as to institute them. If, in the opinion of the people, the distribution or modification of the constitutional powers be in any particular wrong, let it be corrected by an amendment in the way, which the constitution designates—But let there be no change by usurpation; for though this, in one instance, may be the instrument of good, it is the customary weapon by which free governments are destroyed—The precedent must always greatly overbalance in permanent evil any partial or transient benefit which the use can at any time yield.

OF all the dispositions and habits which lead to political prosperity, Religion and Morality are indispensable support. In vain would that man claim the tribute of Patriotism, who would labor to subvert these great pillars of human happiness, these firmest props of the duties of Men and Citizens. The mere politician, equally with the pious Man ought to respect and cherish them —a volume could not trace all their connections with private and public felicity. Let it simply be asked, where is the security for property, for reputation, for life, if the sense of religious obligation *desert* the oaths which are the instruments of investigation in Courts of Justice ? and let us with caution indulge the supposition that morality can be maintained without religion. Whatever may be conceded to the influénce of refined education on minds of peculiar structure ; reason and experience both forbid us to expect that national morality can prevail in exclusion of religious principle.

'Tis substantially true that virtue or morality is a necessary spring of popular government. The rule indeed extends with more or less force to every species of free government. Who that is a sincere Friend to it can look with indifference upon attempts to shake the foundation of the Fabric ?

Promote, then as an object of primary importance institutions for the general diffusion of knowledge. In proportion as the structure of a government gives force to public opinion, it is essential that public opinion should be enlightened.

As a very important source of strength and security, cherish public credit. One method of preserving it is to use it as sparingly as possible; avoiding occasions of expence by cultivating peace, but remembering also that timely disbursments to prepare for dangers, frequently prevent much greater disbursments to repel it; avoiding likewise the accumulation of debt, not only by shunning occasions of expence, but by vigorous exertions in time of peace to discharge the debts which unavoidable Wars may have occasioned, not ungenerously throwing upon posterity the burthen which we ourselves ought to bear. The execution of these Maxims belongs to your Representatives, but it is necessary that public opinion should co-operate. To facilitate to them the performance of their duty, it is essential, that you fhould practically bear in mind, that towards the payment of debts there muft be revenue; that to have Revenue there muft be Taxes; that no Taxes can be devifed which are not more or lefs inconvenient and unpleafant; that the intrinfic embarraffment infeparable from the felection of the proper objects (which is always a choice of difficulties) ought to be a decifive motive for a candid conftruction of the conduct of the government in making it, and for a fpirit of acquiefcence in the meafures for obtaining Revenue which the public exigencies may at any time dictate.

OBSERVE good Faith and Juftice towards all Nations, cultivate peace and harmony with all;—Religion and Morality enjoin this conduct: And can it be that good policy does not equally enjoin it? It will be worthy of a free, enlightened, and at no diftant period, a great Nation, to give to mankind the magnanimous and too novel example of a people always guided by an exalted juftice and benevolence.—Who can doubt that in the courfe of time and things, the fruits of fuch a plan would richly repay any temporary advantages which might be loft by a fteady adhereance to it? Can it be, that Providence has not connected the permanent felicity of a Nation with Virtue? The experiment, at leaft, is recommended by every fentiment which ennobles human nature.—Alas! Is it rendered impoffible by its vices?

IN the execution of fuch a plan, nothing is more effential than that permanent, inveterate antipathies againft particular Nations, and paffionate attachments for others fhould be excluded: And that in place of them juft and amicable feelings towards all fhould be cultivated. The Nation which indulges towards another an habitual hatred, or an habitual fondnefs, is in fome degree a flave. It is a flave to its animofity, or to it affection, either of which is fufficient to lead it aftray from its duty and its intereft. Antipathy in one nation againft another difpofes each more readily to offer infult and injury, to lay hold of flight caufes of umbrage, and to be haughty and untractable, when accidental or trifling occafions of difpute occur. Hence frequent collifions, obftinate, envenomed and bloody contefts. The Nation, prompted by ill will and refentment fometimes impels to war the government, contrary to the beft calculations of policy. The Government fometimes participates in the national propenfity, and adopts through paffion what reafon would reject; at other times, it makes the aimofity of the nation fubfervient to projects of hoftility inftigated by pride, ambition, and other finifter and pernicious motives. The peace often, fometimes perhaps the liberty, of Nations has been the victim.

So likewife, a paffionate attachment of one nation for another, produces a variety of evils. Sympathy for the favourite nation, facilitating this illufion of an imaginary common intereft, in cafes where no real common intereft exifts, and infufing into one the interefts of the other, betrays the former into a participation in the quarrels and wars of the latter, without adequate inducement or juftification. It leads alfo to conceffions to the favourite nation of privileges denied to others, which is apt doubly to injure the nation making the conceffions ; by unneceffarily parting with what ought to have been retained ; and by exciting jealoufy, ill will, and a difpofition to retaliate, in the parties from whom equal privileges are withheld : And it gives to ambitious, corrupted, or deluded citizens (who devote themfelves to the favourite nation) facility to betray, or facrifice the interefts of their own country, without odium,— fometimes even with popularity : Gilding with the appearances of a virtuous fenfe of obligation a commendable deference for public opinion, or a laudable zeal for public good, the bafe or foolifh compliances of ambition, corruption or infatuation.

As avenues to foreign influence in innumerable ways, fuch attachments are particularly alarming to the truly enlightened and independent patriot. How many opportunities do they afford to tamper with domeftic factions, to practice the arts of feduction, to miflead public opinion, to influence or awe the public councils !—Such an attachment of a fmall or weak, towards a great and powerful nation, dooms the former to be the fatelite of the latter.

AGAINST the infidious wiles of foreign influence (I conjure you to believe me, fellow-citizens) the jealoufy of a free people, ought to be *conftantly* awake ; fince hiftory and experience prove that foreign influence is one of the moft baneful foes of republican government. But that jealousy to be useful, must be impartial; else it becomes the instrument of the very influence to be avoided, instead of a defence against it. Excessive partiality for one foreign nation, and excessive dislike of another, cause those whom they actuate to see danger only on one side, and serve to veil and even second the arts of influence on the other.—Real patriots, who may resist the intrigues of the favourite, are liable to become suspected and odious; while its tools and dupes usurp the applause and confidence of the people, to surrender their interests.

THE great rule of conduct for us, in regard to foreign nations, is in extending our commercial relations, to have with them as little *political* connection as possible. So far as we have already formed engagements, let them be fulfilled with perfect good faith. Here let us stop.

EUROPE has a set of primary interests, which to us have none, or a very remote relation. Hence she must be engaged in frequent controversies, the causes of which are essentially foreign to our concerns. Hence, therefore, it must be unwise in us to implicate ourselves, by artificial ties, in the ordinary vicissitudes of her politics, or the ordinary combinations and collisions of her friendships, or enmities.

OUR detached and distant situation, invites and enables us to pursue a different course. If we remain one people, under an efficient government, the period is not far off, when we may defy material injury from external annoyance; when we may take such an attitude as will cause the neutrality, we may at any time resolve upon, to be scrupulously respected; when belligerent nations, under the impossibility of making acquisitions upon us, will not lightly hazard the giving us provocations; when we may chuse peace or war, as our interest, guided by justice, shall counsel.

WHY forego the advantages of so peculiar a situation? Why quit our own, to stand upon foreign ground? Why, by interweaving our destiny with that of any part of Europe, entangle our peace and prosperity in the toils of European ambition, rivalship, interest, humour, or caprice?

'TIS our true policy to steer clear of permanent alliances, with any portion of the foreign world; so far, I mean,

as we are now at liberty to do it; for let me not be understood as capable of patronising infidelity to existing engagements. I hold the maxim no less applicable to public than
to private affairs, that honesty is always the best policy.
I repeat it, therefore, let those engagements be observed in
their genuine sense. But, in my opinion, it is unnecessary,
and would be unwise to extend them.

TAKING care always to keep ourselves, by suitable establishments, on a respectable defensive posture, we may
safely trust to temporary alliances for extradordinary emer-
gencies.

HARMONY, liberal intercourse with all nations, are recommended by policy, humanity, and interest. But even
our commercial policy should hold an equal and impartial
hand; neither sending or granting exclusive favours or pre-
ferences; consulting the natural course of things; diffusing
and diversifying by gentle means the streams of commerce,
but forcing nothing; establishing, with powers so disposed,
in order to give our trade a stable course, to define the rights
of our merchants, and to enable the government to support
them; conventional rules of intercourse, the best that present circumstances and mutual opinion will permit, but temporary, and liable to be from time to time abandoned or
varied, as experience and circumstances shall dictate; constantly keeping in view, that 'tis folly in one nation to look
for disinterested favours from another; that it must pay
with a portion of its independence for whatever it may accept under that character; that by such acceptance, it may
place itself in the condition of having given equivalents for
nominal favours, and yet of being reproached with ingra-
titude for not giving more. There can be no greater error
than to expect, or calculate, upon real favours from nation
to nation.———'Tis an illusion which experience must cure,
which a just pride ought to discard.

IN offering to you, my countrymen, these counsels of
an old and affectionate friend, I dare not hope they will
make the strong and lasting impression I could wish—that
they will controul the usual current of the passions, or prevent our nation from running the course which has hitherto
marked the destiny of nations:—But if I may even flatter
myself, that they may be productive of some partial benefit,

some occasional good; that they may now and then recur to moderate the fury of party spirit, to warn against the mischiefs of foreign intrigue, to guard against the impostures of pretended patriotism; this hope will be a full recompence for the solicitude for your welfare, by which they have been dictated.

How far in the discharge of my official duties, I have been guided by the principles which have been delineated, the public records and other evidences of my conduct must witness to you and to the world. To myself, the assurance of my own conscience is, that I have at least believed myself to be guided by them.

In relation to the still subsisting war in Europe, my Proclamation of the 22d of April 1793, is the index to my plan. Sanctioned by your approving voice, and by that of your Representatives in both Houses of Congress, the spirit of that measure has continually governed me; uninfluenced by any attempts to deter or divert me from it.

After deliberate examination with the aid of the best lights I could obtain, I was well satisfied that our country, under all the circumstances of the case, had a right to take, and was bound in duty and interest, to take a neutral position. Having taken it, I determined, as far as should depend upon me, to maintain it, with moderation.

The considerations which respect the right to hold this conduct, it is not necessary on this occasion to detail. I will only observe, that according to my understanding of the matter, that right, so far from being denied by any of the Belligerent Powers, has been virtually admitted by all.

The duty of holding a neutral conduct may be inferred, without any thing more, from the obligation which justice and humanity impose on every nation, in cases in which it is free to act, to maintain inviolate the relations of peace and amity towards other nations.

The inducements of interest for observing that conduct will best be referred to your own reflections and experience. With me, a predominant motive has been to endeavour to gain time to our country to settle and mature its yet recent institutions, and to progress without interruption, to that degree of strength and consistency, which is necessary to give it, humanly speaking, the command of its own fortunes.

Though in reviewing the incidents of my administration, I am unconscious of intentional error; I am nevertheless too sensible of my defects not to think it probable that I may have committed many errors. Whatever they may be I fervently beseech the Almighty to avert or mitigate the evils to which they may tend. I shall always carry with me the hope that my country will never cease to view them with indulgence; and that after forty-five years of my life dedicated to its service, with an upright zeal, the faults of incompetent abilities will be consigned to oblivion, as myself must soon be to the mansions of rest.

Relying on its kindness in this as in other things, and actuated by that fervent love toward it, which is so natural to a man who views in it the native soil of himself and his progenitors for several generations; I anticipate with pleasing expectation that retreat, in which I promise myself to realize, without alloy, the sweet enjoyment of partaking in the midst of my fellow citizens, the benign influence of good laws under a free government—the ever favourite object of my heart, and the happy reward, as I trust, of our mutual cares, labours and dangers.

United States, 17th September, 1796.   GEO: WASHINGTON.

THOMAS JEFFERSON

Thomas Jefferson

Inaugural Address, 1801

THE TONE of Jefferson's inaugural address was most felicitous, surprising supporters and opponents alike. It was perhaps Jefferson's most masterly public utterance. The decade preceding his inauguration had been marked by party rivalry, so bitter that Washington in his Farewell Address had inveighed against it. But it had gathered force during the Adams administration. For the moment at least, Jefferson rose high above party politics. He spoke of efforts for the common good, the sanctity of the constitution, the equality of law, and the rights of minorities. Without harmony and affection, he urged, even liberty would be a dreary thing. He praised the republican form of government as the world's best hope and urged devotion to the union and to democratic government, friendship with all nations and entangling alliances with none. He praised the liberties that all Americans were privileged to enjoy. Thus Jefferson, in this first inaugural, shed his partisan shackles and spoke as the statesman whose memory is revered by all Americans.

This is a facsimile of an early edition of the Address printed by H. Sprague, Boston, 1802.

Thomas Jefferſon's Speech.

Waſhington, March 4, 1801.

FRIENDS AND FELLOW CITIZENS,

CALLED upon to undertake the duties of the firſt Executive office of our country, I avail myſelf of the preſence of that portion of my fellow-citizens which is here aſſembled, to expreſs my grateful thanks for the favour with which they have been pleaſed to look towards me, to declare a ſincere conſciouſneſs that the taſk is above my talents, and that I approach it with thoſe anxious and awful preſentiments which the greatneſs of the charge, and the weakneſs of my powers ſo juſtly inſpire. A riſing nation, ſpread over a wide and fruitful land, traverſing all the ſeas with the rich productions of their induſtry, engaged in commerce with nations who feel power and forget right, advancing rapidly to deftinies beyond the reach of mortal eye ; when I contemplate thefe tranfcendent objects, and fee the honour, the happinefs, and the hopes of this beloved country committed to the iffue and the aufpices of this day, I fhrink from the contemplation, and humble my-felf before the magnitude of the undertak-ing. Utterly indeed fhould I defpair, did not the prefence of many, whom I here fee, remind me, that, in the other high authorities provided by our conftitu-tion, I fhall find refources of wifdom, of virtue, and of zeal, on which to rely un-der all difficulties. To you, then, gentle-men, who are charged with the fovereign functions of legiflation, and to thofe affoci-ated with you, I look with encouragement for that guidance and fupport which may enable us to fteer with fafety the veffel in which we are all embarked, amidft the conflicting elements of a troubled world,

During the conteſt of opinion through which we have paſt, the animation of diſcuſſions and of exertions has ſometimes worn an aſpect which might impoſe on ſtrangers unuſed to think freely, and to ſpeak and to write what they think ; but this being now decided by the voice of the nation announced according to the rules of the conſtitution, all will of courſe arrange themſelves under the will of the law, and unite in common efforts for the common good. All too will bear in mind this ſacred principle, that though the will of the majority is in all caſes to prevail, that will, to be rightful, muſt be reaſonable ; that the minority poſſeſs their equal rights, which equal laws muſt protect, and to violate would be oppreſſion. Let us then, fellow-citizens, unite, with one heart and one mind, let us reſtore to ſocial intercourſe that harmony and affection without which liberty, and even life itſelf, are but dreary things.——And let us reflect that having banifhed from our land that religious intolerance under which mankind fo long bled and fuffered, we have yet gained little, if we countenance a political intolerance, as defpotic, as wicked, and capable of as bitter and bloody perfecutions.   During the throes and convulfions of the ancient world, during the agonizing fpafms of infuriated man, feeking through blood and flaughter his long loft liberty, it was not wonderful that the agitation of the billows fhould reach even this diftant and peaceful fhore; that this fhould be more felt & feared by fome, and lefs by others ; and fhould divide opinions as to meafures of fafety; but every difference of opinion is not a difference of principle.   We have called by different names brethren of the fame principle.   We are all republicans : we are all federalifts.   If there be any among us who would wifh to diffolve this Union, or to change its republican form, let them

ſtanſt undiſturbed as monuments of the
ſafety with which error of opinion may
be tolerated, where reaſon is left free to
combat it. I know indeed that ſome
honeſt men fear that a republican government cannot be ſtrong; that this government is not ſtrong enough. But
would the honeſt patriot, in the full tide
of ſucceſsful experiment, abandon a government which has ſo far kept us free
and firm, on the theoretic and viſionary
fear, that this government, the world's
beſt hope, may, by poſſibility, want energy to preſerve itſelf? I truſt not. I believe this, on the contrary, the ſtrongeſt
government on earth. I believe it the
only one, where every man, at the call of
the law, would fly to the ſtandard of the
law, and would meet invaſions of the
public order as his own perſonal concern.
Sometimes it is ſaid that man cannot be
truſted with the government of himſelf.
Can he then be truſted with the govern-

E

ment of others? Or have we found angels, in the form of kings, to govern
him? Let hiftory anfwer this queftion.

Let us then, with courage and confidence, purfue our own federal and republican principles ; our attachment to union
and reprefentative government. Kindly
feparated by nature and a wide ocean
from the exterminating havoc of one quarter of the globe ; too high minded to endure the degradations of the others, poffef-
fing a chofen country, with room enough
for our defcendants to the thoufandth and
thoufandth generation, entertaining a due
fenfe of our equal right to the ufe of our
own faculties, to the acquifitions of our
own induftry, to honor and confidence
from our fellow-citizens, refulting not
from birth, but from our actions and
their fenfe of them, enlightened by a benign religion, profeffed indeed and prac-
ifed in various forms, yet all of them in-
culcating honefty, truth, temperance,

gratitude and the love of man, acknowl-
edging and adoring an overruling Providence, which by all its difpenfations proves
that it delights in the happinefs of man
here, and his greater happinefs hereafter;
with all thefe bleffings, what more is neceffary to make us a happy and a prof-
perous people? Still one thing more, fellow-citizens, a wife and frugal government, which fhall reftrain men from in-
juring one another, fhall leave them otherwife free to regulate their own purfuits
of induftry and improvement, and fhall
not take from the mouth of labor the
bread it has earned. This is the fum of
good government; and this is neceffary
to clofe the circle of our felicities.

About to enter, fellow-citizens, on the
exercife of duties which comprehend every thing dear and valuable to you, it is
proper you fhould underftand what I
deem the effential principles of our government, and confequently thofe which

ought to fhape its adminiftration. I will comprefs them within the narroweft compafs they will bear, ftating the general principle, but not all its luminations.— equal and exact juftice to all men, of whatever ftate or perfuafion, religious or political :—peace, commerce, and honeft friendfhip with all nations, entangling alliances with none :—the fupport of the ftate governments in all their rights, as the moft competent adminiftrations for our domeftic concerns, and the fureft bulwark againft anti-republican tendencies: the prefervation of the general government in its whole conftitutional vigor, as the fheet anchorof ourpeaceat home, andfafetyabroad: a jealous care of the right of election by the people, a mild and fafe corrective of abufes which are lopped by the fword of revolution, where peaceable remedies are unprovided :—abfolute acquiefcence in the decifions of the majority, the vital principle of republics, from which is no appeal but to force, the vital principle and immediate parent of defpotifm :—a well difciplined militia, our beft reliance in peace, and for the firft moments of war, till regulars may relieve them :— the fupremacy of the civil over the military authority :—economy in the public expence, that labor may be lightly burthened :—the honeft payment of our debts, and facred prefervation of the public faith :—encouragement of agriculture, and of commerce as its hand maid :— the diffufion of information, and arraignment of all abufes at the bar of the public reafon :—freedom of religion ; freedom of the prefs ; and freedom of perfon, under the protection of the Habeas Corpus :—and trial by juries impartially felected.—Thefe principles form the bright conftellation, which has gone before us, and guided our fteps throught an age of revolution and reformation. The wifdom of our fages, and blood of our heroes,

have been devoted to their attainment :—
they should be the creed of our political
faith; the text of civic instruction, the
touchstone by which to try the services of
those we trust; and should we wander from
them in moments of error or of alarm, let us
ten to retrace our steps, and to regain the
road which alone leads to peace, liberty
and safety.

I repair then, fellow-citizens, to the
post you have assigned me. With experience enough in subordinate offices to
have seen the difficulties of this the greatest of all, I have learnt to expect that it
will rarely fall to the lot of imperfect man
to retire from this station with the reputation, and the favor, which bring him into it. Without pretentions to that high
confidence you reposed in your first and
greatest revolutionary character, whose
pre-eminent services had entitled him to
the first place in his country's love, and
destined for him the fairest page in the

volume of faithful hiftory, I afk fo much confidence only as may give firmnefs and effect to the legal adminiftration of your affairs. I fhall often go wrong through defect of judgment. When right, I fhall often be thought wrong by thofe whofe pofitions will not command a view of the whole ground. I afk your indulgence for my own errors, which will never be intentional ; and your fupport againft the errors of others, who may condemn what they would not, if feen in all its parts. The approbation implied by your fuffrage, is a great confolation to me for the paft ; and my future folicitude will be, to retain the good opinion of thofe who have be- ftowed it in advance, to conciliate that of others, by doing them all the good in my power, and to be inftrumental in the hap- pinefs and freedom of all.

Relying then on the patronage of your good will, I advance with obedience to the work, ready to retire from it whenever you become fenfible how much better choices it is in your power to make. And may that infinite Power, which rules the deftinies of the univerfe, lead our councils to what is beft, and give them a favorable iffue for your peace and profperity.

JAMES MADISON

James Madison

The War Message, 1812

PRESIDENT MADISON's special message to Congress is dated June 1, 1812, and Congress declared war against England on June 18. Madison wearily cited the impressment of American seamen, the interference with American trade on the high seas, and British incitement of the Indians against the frontier settlements as ample reasons for going to war. The expansionist War Hawks from the West and the South needed no prodding to act upon the President's message, although the vote against declaring war was substantial. The New England representatives, whom one would naturally expect to resent British interference with commerce, were opposed to war. They were, of course, Federalists; but, more important, they regarded England as a bulwark against Napoleon, the Antichrist who had duped the President by commitments he did not intend to keep. Oddly enough, unaware of the American declaration, a new British ministry had repealed the obnoxious Orders in Council. Writing in 1813, Thomas Jefferson, who had himself as president struggled with these problems, vigorously upheld Madison. In the light of continued provocation by Great Britain, the former President concluded that "no alternative remained but war, or the abandonment of the persons and property of our citizens on the ocean."

The facsimile is that of the "Message from the President of the U. States, recommending an immediate declaration of war, against Great Britain," an official document printed in 1812 by Roger C. Weightmen at Washington.

MESSAGE.

To the Senate and House of Representatives of the United States.

I COMMUNICATE to Congress certain documents, being a continuation of those heretofore laid before them, on the subject of our affairs with Great Britain.

Without going back beyond the renewal in 1803, of the war in which Great Britain is engaged, and omitting unrepaired wrongs of inferior magnitude, the conduct of her government presents a series of acts, hostile to the United States as an independent and neutral nation.

British cruizers have been in the continued practice of violating the American flag on the great high way of nations, and of seizing and carrying off persons sailing under it; not in the exercise of a belligerent right, founded on the law of nations against an enemy, but of a municipal prerogative over British subjects. British jurisdiction is thus extended to neutral vessels, in a situation where no laws can operate but the law of nations, and the laws of the country to which the vessels belong; and a self redress is assumed, which, if British subjects were wrongfully detained and alone concerned, is that substitution of force, for a resort to the responsible sovereign, which falls within the definition of war. Could the seizure of British subjects, in such cases, be regarded as within the exercise of a belligerent right, the acknowledged laws of war, which forbid an article of captured property to be adjudged, without a regular investigation before a competent tribunal, would imperiously demand the fairest trial, where the sacred rights of persons were at issue In place of such a trial, these rights are subjected to the will of every petty commander.

The practice, hence, is so far from affecting British subjects alone, that under the pretext of searching for these, thousands of American citizens, under the safeguard of public law, and of their national flag, have been torn from their country, and from every thing dear to them; have been dragged on board ships of war of a foreign nation, and exposed under the severities of their discipline, to be exiled to the most distant and deadly climes, to risk their lives in the battles of their oppressors, and to be the melancholy instruments of taking away those of their own brethren.

Against this crying enormity, which Great Britain would be so prompt to avenge if committed against herself, the United States have in vain exhausted remonstrances and expostulations; and that no proof might be wanting of their conciliatory dispositions, and no pretext left for a continuance of the practice, the British government was formally assured of the readiness of the United States to enter into arrangements, such as could not be rejected, if the recovery of British subjects were the real and the sole object. The communication passed without effect.

British cruizers have been in the practice also of violating the rights and the peace of our coasts. They hover over and harrass our entering and departing commerce. To the most insulting pretensions they have added the most lawless proceedings in our very harbors; and have wantonly spilt American blood within the sanctuary of our territorial jurisdiction. The principles and rules enforced by that nation when a neutral nation, against armed vessels of belligerents hovering near her coasts and disturbing her commerce, are well known. When called on, nevertheless. by the United States, to punish the greater offences committed by her own vessels, her government has bestowed on their commanders additional marks of honor and confidence.

Under pretended blockades, without the presence of an adequate force, and sometimes without the practicability of applying one, our commerce has been plundered in every sea; the great staples of our country have been cut off from their legitimate markets; and a destructive blow aimed at our agricultural and maritime interests. In aggravation of these predatory measures, they have been considered as in force from the dates of their notification; a retrospective effect being thus added, as has been done in other important cases, to the unlawfulness of the course pursued. And to render the outrage the more signal, these mock blockades have been reiterated and enforced in the face of official communications from the British government, declaring, as the true definition of a legal blockade, " that particular ports must be actually invested, and previous warning given to vessels bound to them, not to enter."

Not content with these occasional expedients for laying waste our neutral trade, the cabinet of Great Britain resorted, at length, to the sweeping system of blockades, under the name of orders in council; which has been moulded and managed, as might best suit its political views, its commercial jealousies, or the avidity of British cruizers.

To our remonstrances against the complicated and transcendant injustice of this innovotion, the first reply was, that the orders were reluctantly adopted by Great Britain, as a necessary retaliation on decrees of her enemy, proclaiming a general blockade of the British isles, at a time when the naval force of that enemy dared not to issue from his own ports She was reminded, without effect, that her own prior blockades, unsupported by an adequate naval force actually applied and continued, were a bar to this plea: that executed edicts against millions of our property could not be retaliation on edicts, confessedly impossible to be executed: that retaliation to be just, should fall on the party setting the guilty example, not on an innocent party, which was not even chargeable with an acquiescence in it.

When deprived of this flimsy veil for a prohibition of our trade with her enemy, by the repeal of his prohibition of our trade with Great Britain, her cabinet, instead of a corresponding repeal, or a practical discontinuance of its orders, formally avowed a determination to persist in them against the United States, until the markets of her enemy should be laid open to British products; thus, asserting an obligation on a neutral power to require one belligerent to encourage, by its internal regulations, the trade of another belligerent; contradicting her own practice towards all nations, in peace as well as in war; and betraying the insincerity of those professions which inculcated a belief, that having resorted to her orders with regret, she was anxious to find an occasion for putting an end to them

Abandoning, still more, all respect for the neutral rights of the United States, and for its own consistency, the British government now demands, as pre requisites to a repeal of its orders as they relate to the United States, that a formality should be observed in the repeal of the French decrees, no wise necessary to their termination, nor exemplified by British usage; and that the

French repeal, besides including that portion of the decrees which operate within a territorial jurisdiction, as well as that which operates on the high seas, against the commerce of the United States, should not be a single and special repeal in relation to the United States, but should be extended to whatever other neutral nations, unconnected with them, may be affected by those decrees. And, as an additional insult, they are called on for a formal disavowal of conditions and pretensions advanced by the French government, for which the United States are so far from having made themselves responsible, that in official explanations, which have been published to the world, and in a correspondence of the American Minister at London with the British Minister for Foreign Affairs, such a responsibility was explicitly and emphatically disclaimed.

It has become, indeed, sufficiently certain, that the commerce of the United States is to be sacrificed, not as interfering with the belligerent rights of Great Britain; not as supplying the wants of her enemies, which she herself supplies; but, as interfering with the monopoly which she covets for her own commerce and navigation. She carries on a war against the lawful commerce of a friend, that she may the better carry on a commerce with an enemy; a commerce polluted by the forgeries and perjuries, which are, for the most part, the only passports by which it can succeed

Anxious to make every experiment, short of the last resort of injured nations, the United States have withheld from Great Britain, under successive modifications, the benefits of a free intercourse with their market, the loss of which could not but outweigh the profits accruing from her restrictions of our commerce with other nations. And to entitle these experiments to the more favorable consideration, they were so framed as to enable her to place her adversary under the exclusive operation of them To these appeals her government has been equally inflexible, as if willing to make sacrifices of every sort, rather than yield to the claims of justice, or renounce the errors of a false pride Nay, so far were the attempts carried to overcome the attachment of the British cabinet to its unjust edicts, that it received every encouragement within the competency of the executive branch of our government, to expect that a repeal of them would be followed by a war between the United States and France, unless the French edicts should also be repealed Even this communication, although silencing forever the plea of a disposition in the United States to acquiesce in those edicts, originally the sole plea for them, received no attention.

If no other proof existed of a predetermination of the British government against a repeal of its orders, it might be found in the correspondence of the Minister Plenipotentiary of the United States at London and the British Secretary for Foreign Affairs, in 1810, on the question whether the blockade of May, 1806, was considered as in force, or as not in force. It had been ascertained that the French government, which urged this blockade as the ground of its Berlin decree, was willing, in the event of its removal, to repeal that decree; which being followed by alternate repeals of the other offensive edicts, might abolish the whole system on both sides. This inviting opportunity for accomplishing an object so important to the United States, and professed so often to be the desire of both the belligerents, was made known to the British government. As that government admits that an actual application of an adequate force, is necessary to the existence of a legal blockade, and it was notorious, that if such a force had ever been applied, its long discontinuance had annulled the blockade in question, there could be no sufficient objection on the part of Great Britain to a formal revocation of it; and no imaginable objection to a declaration of the fact, that the blockade did not exist. The declaration would have been consistent with her avowed principles of blockade; and would have enabled the United States to demand from France the pledged repeal of her decrees; either with success, in which case the way would have been opened for a general repeal of the belligerent edicts; or without success, in which case the United States would have been justified in turning their measures exclusively against France. The British government would, however, neither rescind the blockade, nor declare its non existence; nor permit its non existence to be inferred and affirmed by the American plenipotentiary. On the contrary, by representing the blockade to be comprehended in the orders in council, the United States were compelled so to regard it, in their subsequent proceedings.

There was a period when a favorable change in the policy of the British cabinet, was justly considered as established. The Minister Plenipotentiary of his Britannic Majesty here, proposed an adjustment of the differences more immediately endangering the harmony of the two countries. The proposition was accepted with the promptitude and cordiality, corresponding with the invariable professions of this government. A foundation appeared to be laid for a sincere and lasting reconciliation. The prospect, however quickly vanished The whole proceeding was disavowed by the British government without any explanations, which could. at that time, repress the belief, that the disavowal proceeded from a spirit of hostility to the commercial

2

rights and prosperity of the United States. And it has since come into proof that at the very moment, when the public minister was holding the language of friendship, and inspiring confidence in the sincerity of the negotiation with which he was charged, a secret agent of his government was employed in intrigues, having for their object, a subversion of our government, and a dismemberment of our happy Union.

In reviewing the conduct of Great Britain towards the United States, our attention is necessarily drawn to the warfare, just renewed by the savages, on one of our extensive frontiers ; a warfare, which is known to spare neither age nor sex, and to be distinguished by features peculiarly shocking to humanity. It is difficult to account for the activity and combinations which have for some time been developing themselves among tribes in constant intercourse with British traders and garrisons, without connecting their hostility with that influence, and without recollecting the authenticated examples of such interpositions, heretofore furnished by the officers and agents of that government.

Such is the spectacle of injuries and indignities, which have been heaped on our country ; and such the crisis which its unexampled forbearance and conciliatory efforts, have not been able to avert. It might, at least have been expected, that an enlightened nation, if less urged by moral obligations, or invited by friendly dispositions on the part of the United States, would have found, in its true interest alone, a sufficient motive to respect their rights and their tranquillity on the high seas: that an enlarged policy would have favored that free and general circulation of commerce in which the British nation is at all times interested, and which, in times of war, is the best alleviation of its calamities to herself, as well as to other belligerents; and, more especially, that the British cabinet, would not, for the sake of a precarious and surreptitious intercourse with hostile markets, have persevered in a course of measures, which necessarily put at hazard the invaluable market of a great and growing country, disposed to cultivate the mutual advantages of an active commerce.

Other councils have prevailed. Our moderation and conciliation have had no other effect than to encourage perseverance and to enlarge pretensions. We behold our seafaring citizens still the daily victims of lawless violence, committed on the great common and highway of nations, even within sight of the country which owes them protection. We behold our vessels, freighted with the products of our soil and industry, or returning with the honest proceeds of them, wrested from their lawful destinations, confiscated by prize courts, no longer the organs of public law, but the instruments of arbitrary edicts; and their unfortunate crews dispersed and lost, or forced or inveigled in British ports into British fleets; whilst arguments are employed, in support of these aggressions, which have no foundation but in a principle, equally supporting a claim to regulate our external commerce, in all cases whatsoever.

We behold, in fine, on the side of Great Britain, a state of war against the United States; and on the side of the United States, a state of peace towards Great Britain.

Whether the United States shall continue passive under these progressive usurpations, and these accumulating wrongs; or, opposing force to force in defence of their national rights, shall commit a just cause into the hands of the Almighty Disposer of events; avoiding all connections which might entangle it in the contests or views of other powers, and preserving a constant readiness to concur in an honorable re establishment of peace and friendship, is a solemn question, which the constitution wisely confides to the legislative department of the government. In recommending it to their early deliberations, I am happy in the assurance, that the decision will be worthy the enlightened and patriotic councils of a virtuous, a free, and a powerful nation.

Having presented this view of the relations of the United States with Great Britain, and of the solemn alternative growing out of them, I proceed to remark that the communications last made to Congress on the subject of our relations with France, will have shewn, that since the revocation of her decrees, as they violated the neutral rights of the United States, her government has authorised illegal captures by its privateers and public ships; and that other outrages have been practised on our vessels and our citizens. It will have been seen, also, that no indemnity had been provided, or satisfactorily pledged, for the extensive spoliations, committed under the violent and retrospective orders of the French government against the property of our citizens, seized within the jurisdiction of France. I abstain, at this time, from recommending to the consideration of Congress definitive measures with respect to that nation, in the expectation, that the result of unclosed discussions between our minister plenipotentiary at Paris and the French government, will speedily enable Congress to decide, with greater advantage, on the course due to the rights, the interests, and the honor of our country.

JAMES MADISON.

Washington, June 1, 1812.

JAMES MONROE

James Monroe

The Monroe Doctrine, 1823

THE MONROE DOCTRINE is a strange document with an odd origin and an unending later history. As a document it consists of only three paragraphs, buried in two separated places in President Monroe's otherwise routine Seventh Annual Message to Congress. The prohibition on European colonization is developed in one place, while the concept of an American hemisphere from which the autocratic European political system would be forever debarred is expounded in another.

In 1823 the Holy Alliance threatened to restore to Spain the Latin American countries that had won independence. The United States, aware of the great stake of the British merchants in the new Latin American trade, first worked for a joint Anglo-American declaration as a means of meeting this danger. But Britain finally demurred, persuading herself that the United States coveted Cuba! At this juncture John Quincy Adams, our Secretary of State, and others, urged the President to make a solely American pronouncement. President Monroe's pronouncements were practically ignored in Europe when they were published, indeed it was not until the Civil War that they became generally known as a doctrine.

These excerpts are reproduced from the President's Message of December 2, 1823, which is listed as Document 2, Eighteenth Congress, First Session. It was printed at Washington by Gales and Seaton in 1823. A copy was kindly lent by the Library of the University of California at Los Angeles.

JAMES MONROE
THE MONROE DOCTRINE
from the Message to Congress, December 2, 1823

. . . .

At the proposal of the Russian imperial government, made through the minister of the Emperor residing here, a full power and instructions have been transmitted to the Minister of the United States at St. Peterburgh, to arrange, by amicable negotiation, the respective rights and interests of the two nations on the northwest coast of this continent. A similar proposal has been made by his Imperial Majesty to the government of Great Britain, which has likewise been acceded to. The government of the United States has been desirous, by this friendly proceeding, of manifesting the great value which they have invariably attached to the friendship of the emperor, and their solicitude to cultivate the best understanding with his goverment. In the discussions to which this interest has given rise, and in the arrangements by which they may terminate, the occasion has been judged proper for asserting, as a principle in which the rights and interests of the United States are involved, that the American continents, by the free and independent condition which they have assumed and maintain, are henceforth not to be considered as subjects for future colonization by any European powers.

. . . .

It was stated at the commencement of the last session, that a great effort was then making in Spain and Portugal, to improve the condition of the people of those countries, and that it appeared to be conducted with extraordinary moderation. It need scarcely be remarked, that the result has been, so far, very different from what was then anticipated. Of events in that quarter of the globe, with which we have so much intercourse, and from which we derive our origin, we have always been anxious and interested spectators. The citizens of the United States cherish sentiments the most friendly, in favor of the liberty and happiness of their fellow men on that side of the Atlantic. In the wars of the European powers, in matters relating to themselves, we have never taken any part, nor does it comport with our policy so to do. It is only when our rights are invaded, or seriously menaced, that we resent injuries, or make preparation for our defence. With the movements in this hemisphere, we are, of necessity, more immediately connected, and by causes which must be obvious to all enlightened and impartial observers. The political system of the allied powers is essentially different, in this respect, from that of America. This difference proceeds from that which exists in their respective governments. And to the defence of our own, which has been achieved by the loss of so much blood and treasure, and matured by the wisdom of their most enlightened citizens, and under which we have enjoyed unexampled felicity, this whole nation is devoted. We owe it, therefore, to candor, and to the amicable relations existing between the United States and those powers, to declare, that we should consider any attempt on their part to extend their system to any portion of this hemisphere, as dangerous to our peace and safety. With the existing colonies or dependencies of any European power, we have not interfered, and shall not interfere. But, with the governments who have declared their independence, and maintained it, and whose independence we have, on great consideration, and on just principles, acknowledged, we could not view any interposition for the purpose of oppressing them, or controlling, in any other manner, their destiny, by any European power, in any other light than as the manifestation of an unfriendly disposition towards the United States. In the war between these new governments and Spain, we declared our neutrality at the time of their recognition, and to this we have adhered, and shall continue to adhere, provided no change shall occur, which, in the judgment of the competent authorities of this government, shall make a corresponding change, on the part of the United States, indispensable to their security.

The late events in Spain and Portugal, shew that Europe is still unsettled. Of this important fact, no stronger proof can be adduced than that the allied powers should have thought it proper, on any principle satisfactory to themselves, to have interposed, by force, in the internal concerns of Spain. To what extent such interposition may be carried, on the same principle, is a question, in which all independent powers, whose governments differ from theirs, are interested; even those most remote, and surely none more so than the United States. Our policy, in regard to Europe, which was adopted at an early stage of the wars which have so long agitated that quarter of the globe, nevertheless remains the same, which is, not to interfere in the internal concerns of any of its powers; to consider the government *de facto* as the legitimate government for us: to cultivate friendly relations with it, and to preserve those relations by a frank, firm, and manly policy, meeting, in all instances, the just claims of every power; submitting to injuries from none. But, in regard to these continents, circumstances are eminently and conspicuously different. It is impossible that the allied powers should extend their political system to any portion of either continent, without endangering our peace and happiness; nor can any one believe that our Southern Brethren, if left to themselves, would adopt it of their own accord. It is equally impossible, therefore, that we should behold such interposition, in any form, with indifference. If we look to the comparative strength and resources of Spain and those new governments, and their distance from each other, it must be obvious that she can never subdue them. It is still the true policy of the United States, to leave the parties to themselves, in the hope that other powers will pursue the same course.

. . . .

JAMES MONROE.

WASHINGTON. *December* 2. 1823.

Abraham Lincoln

>>>>>>>>>>>>>>>>>>>>>>>>>>><<<<<<<<<<<<<<<<<<<<<<<<<<<

The Inaugurals, 1861, 1865, and the Gettysburg Address, 1863

ABRAHAM LINCOLN was a ready speaker, but while President he made few public addresses. His greatest were his two inaugurals, the Gettysburg Address, and his last speech, that of April 11, 1865, which dealt with reconstruction. His First Inaugural, delivered on March 4, 1861, was conciliatory. Pleading with his fellow countrymen to think calmly, he stressed the need of preserving the Union and denounced secession as anarchy. But even as he spoke the southern states were seceding one by one.

The Gettysburg Address was delivered on the occasion of the dedication of a national cemetery on November 19, 1863. It was not written, as alleged, on the train, but was completed in Washington. Lincoln made some minor changes in Gettysburg. After listening to the two-hour speech of Senator Everett, the audience was tired. Lincoln rose and slowly read his address. The crowd applauded indifferently. Only a few critics glimpsed the literary excellence of his performance; others, for partisan reasons, belittled or denounced it because it contained no expressions of enmity toward the South. But Senator Everett wrote to Lincoln, "I should be glad if I could flatter myself that I came as near the central idea of the occasion in two hours as you did in two minutes."

The Second Inaugural was delivered on March 4, 1865. The War was to end the following month. Instead of reviewing the events of his administration, Lincoln spoke briefly upon a high spiritual level. Like his Gettysburg Address, it achieved a nobility that has rarely been surpassed by any statesman.

All three addresses are facsimiles of the rare first editions. The First Inaugural is "U. S. Senate Executive Document No. 1 Special Session [Thirty-seventh Congress]," and the full title is "Inaugural Address of The President of the United States, on The Fourth of March, 1861." The Second Inaugural is entitled, "Inaugural Address, March 4, 1865," (Washington, 1865). The Gettysburg Address is found on the verso of the page following Senator Everett's speech in the "Address of Hon. Edward Everett, at the consecration of the national cemetery at Gettysburg, 19th November, 1863, with the dedicatory speech of President Lincoln, and the other exercises of the occasion; . . . ," published by Little, Brown and Company of Boston in 1864.

INAUGURAL ADDRESS

OF

THE PRESIDENT OF THE UNITED STATES,

ON

The Fourth of March, 1861.

MARCH 8, 1861.—Ordered to be printed.

FELLOW-CITIZENS OF THE UNITED STATES: In compliance with a custom as old as the Government itself, I appear before you to address you briefly, and to take in your presence the oath prescribed by the Constitution of the United States to be taken by the President "before he enters on the execution of his office."

I do not consider it necessary at present for me to discuss those matters of administration about which there is no special anxiety or excitement.

Apprehension seems to exist among the people of the Southern States that by the accession of a Republican Administration their property and their peace and personal security are to be endangered. There has never been any reasonable cause for such apprehension. Indeed, the most ample evidence to the contrary has all the while existed and been open to their inspection. It is found in nearly all the published speeches of him who now addresses you. I do but quote from one of those speeches when I declare that "I have no purpose, directly or indirectly, to interfere with the institution of slavery in the States where it exists. I believe I have no lawful right to do so, and I have no inclination to do so." Those who nominated and elected me did so with full knowledge that I had made this and many similar declarations, and had never recanted them. And, more than this, they placed in the platform for my acceptance, and as a law to themselves and to me, the clear and emphatic resolution which I now read :

"*Resolved*, That the maintenance inviolate of the rights of the States, and especially the right of each State to order and control its own domestic institutions according to its own judgment exclusively, is essential to that balance of power on which the perfection and endurance of our political fabric depend, and we denounce the lawless invasion by armed force of the soil of any State or Territory, no matter under what pretext, as among the gravest of crimes."

I now reiterate these sentiments ; and, in doing so, I only press upon the public attention the most conclusive evidence of which the case is susceptible, that the property, peace, and security of no section are to be in anywise endangered by the now incoming Administration. I add, too, that all the protection which, consistently with the Constitution and the laws, can be given, will be cheerfully given to all the States when lawfully demanded, for whatever cause—as cheerfully to one section as to another.

There is much controversy about the delivering up of fugitives from service or labor. The clause I now read is as plainly written in the Constitution as any other of its provisions :

"No personheld to service or labor in one State, under the laws thereof, escaping into another, shall, in consequence of any law or regulation therein, be discharged from such service or labor, but shall be delivered up on claim of the party to whom such service or labor may be due."

It is scarcely questioned that this provision was intended by those who made it for the reclaiming of what we call fugitive slaves; and the intention of the law-giver is the law. All members of Congress swear their support to the whole Constitution—to this provision as much as to any other. To the proposition, then, that slaves, whose cases come within the terms of this clause, "shall be delivered up," their oaths are unanimous. Now, if they would make the effort in good temper, could they not, with nearly equal unanimity, frame and pass a law by means of which to keep good that unanimous oath?

There is some difference of opinion whether this clause should be enforced by national or by State authority ; but surely that difference is not a very material one. If the slave is to be surrendered, it can be of but little consequence to him, or to others, by which authority it is done. And should any one, in any case, be content that his oath shall go unkept, on a merely unsubstantial controversy as to *how* it shall be kept ?

Again, in any law upon this subject, ought not all the safeguards of liberty known in civilized and humane jurisprudence to be introduced, so that a free man be not, in any case, surrendered as a slave? And might it not be well at the same time to provide by law for the enforcement of that clause in the Constitution which guarantees that "the citizen of each State shall be entitled to all privileges and immunities of citizens in the several States?"

I take the official oath to-day with no mental reservations, and with no purpose to construe the Constitution or laws by any hypercritical rules. And while I do not choose now to specify particular acts of Congress as proper to be enforced, I do suggest that it will be much safer for all, both in official and private stations, to conform to and abide by all those acts which stand unrepealed, than to violate any of them, trusting to find impunity in having them held to be unconstitutional.

It is seventy-two years since the first inauguration of a President under our National Constitution. During that period fifteen different and greatly-distinguished citizens have, in succession, administered the Executive branch of the Government. They have conducted it through many perils, and generally with great success. Yet, with all this scope of precedent, I now enter upon the same task for the brief constitutional term of four years under great and peculiar difficulty. A disruption of the Federal Union, heretofore only menaced, is now formidably attempted.

I hold that, in contemplation of universal law, and of the Constitution, the Union of these States is perpetual. Perpetuity is implied, if not expressed, in the fundamental law of all National Governments. It is safe to assert that no Government proper ever had a provision in its organic law for its own termination. Continue to execute all the express provisions of our National Constitution, and the Union will endure forever—it being impossible to destroy it except by some action not provided for in the instrument itself.

Again, if the United States be not a Government proper, but an association of States in the nature of contract merely, can it, as a contract, be peaceably unmade by less than all the parties who made it? One party to a contract may violate it—break it, so to speak; but does it not require all to lawfully rescind it?

Descending from these general principles, we find the proposition that, in legal contemplation, the Union is perpetual, confirmed by the history of the Union itself. The Union is much older than the Constitution. It was formed, in fact, by the Articles of Association in 1774. It was matured and continued by the Declaration of Independence in 1776. It was further matured, and the faith of all the then thirteen States expressly plighted and engaged that it should be perpetual, by the Articles of Confederation in 1778. And, finally, in 1787, one of the declared objects for ordaining and establishing the Constitution was " *to form a more perfect union.*"

But if destruction of the Union by one, or by a part only, of the States, be lawfully possible, the Union is *less* perfect than before the Constitution, having lost the vital element of perpetuity.

It follows, from these views, that no State, upon its own mere motion, can lawfully get out of the Union ; that *resolves* and *ordinances* to that effect are legally void ; and that acts of violence, within any State or States, against the authority of the United States, are insurrectionary or revolutionary, according to circumstances.

I, therefore, consider that, in view of the Constitution and the laws, the Union is unbroken, and, to the extent of my ability, I shall take care, as the Constitution itself expressly enjoins upon me, that the laws of the Union be faithfully executed in all the States. Doing this I deem to be only a simple duty on my part; and I shall perform it, so far as practicable, unless my rightful masters, the American people, shall withhold the requisite means, or, in some authoritative manner, direct the contrary. I trust this will not be regarded as a menace, but only as the declared purpose of the Union that it *will* constitutionally defend and maintain itself.

In doing this there needs to be no bloodshed or violence; and there shall be none, unless it be forced upon the national authority. The power confided to me will be used to hold, occupy, and possess the property and places belonging to the Government, and to collect the duties and imposts; but, beyond what may be necessary for these objects, there will be no invasion, no using of force against or among the people anywhere. Where hostility to the United States, in any interior locality, shall be so great and universal as to prevent competent resident citizens from holding the federal offices, there will be no attempt to force obnoxious strangers among the people for that object. While the strict legal right may exist in the Government to enforce the exercise of these offices, the attempt to do so would be so irritating, and so nearly impracticable withal, that I deem it better to forego, for the time, the uses of such offices.

The mails, unless repelled, will continue to be furnished in all parts of the Union. So far as possible, the people everywhere shall have that sense of perfect security which is most favorable to calm thought and reflection. The course here indicated will be followed, unless current events and experience shall show a modification or change to be proper, and in every case and exigency my best discretion will be exercised, according to circumstances actually existing, and with a view and a hope of a peaceful solution of the national troubles, and the restoration of fraternal sympathies and affections.

That there are persons in one section or another who seek to destroy the Union at all events, and are glad of any pretext to do it, I will neither affirm nor deny; but if there be such, I need address no word to them. To those, however, who really love the Union, may I not speak?

Before entering upon so grave a matter as the destruction of our national fabric, with all its benefits, its memories, and its hopes, would it not be wise to ascertain precisely why we do it? Will you hazard so desperate a step while there is any possibility that any portion of the ills you fly from have no real existence? Will you, while the certain ills you fly to are greater than all the real ones you fly from—will you risk the commission of so fearful a mistake?

All profess to be content in the Union, if all constitutional rights can be maintained. Is it true, then, that any right, plainly written in the Constitution, has been denied? I think not. Happily the human mind is so constituted that no party can reach to the audacity of doing this. Think, if you can, of a single instance in which a plainly written provision of the Constitution has ever been denied. If, by the mere force of numbers, a majority should deprive a minority of any clearly written constitutional right, it might, in a moral point of view, justify revolution—certainly would, if such right were a vital one. But such is not our case. All the vital rights of minorities and of individuals are so plainly assured to them by affirmations and negations, guarantees and prohibitions, in the Constitution, that controversies never arise concerning them. But no organic law can ever be framed with a provision specifically applicable to every question which may occur in practical administration. No foresight can anticipate, nor any document of reasonable length contain, express provisions for all possible questions. Shall fugitives from labor be surrendered by national or by State authority? The Constitution does not expressly say. *May* Congress prohibit slavery in the Territories? The Constitution does not expressly say. *Must* Congress protect slavery in the Territories? The Constitution does not expressly say.

From questions of this class spring all our constitutional controversies, and we divide upon them into majorities and minorities. If the minority will not acquiesce, the majority must, or the Government must cease. There is no other alternative; for continuing the Government is acquiescence on one side or the other. If a minority in such case will secede rather than acquiesce, they make a precedent which in turn will divide and ruin them; for a minority of their own will secede from them whenever a majority refuses to be controlled by such minority. For instance, why may not any portion of a new confederacy, a year or two hence, arbitrarily secede again, precisely as portions of the present Union now claim to secede from it? All who cherish disunion sentiments are now being educated to the exact temper of doing this.

Is there such perfect identity of interests among the States to compose a new Union as to produce harmony only and prevent renewed secession?

Plainly, the central idea of secession is the essence of anarchy. A majority held in restraint by constitutional checks and limitations, and always changing easily with deliberate changes of popular opinions and sentiments, is the only true sovereign of a free people. Whoever rejects it does, of necessity, fly to anarchy or to despotism. Unanimity is impossible; the rule of a minority, as a permanent arrangement, is wholly inadmissible; so that, rejecting the majority principle, anarchy or despotism in some form is all that is left.

I do not forget the position assumed by some, that constitutional questions are to be decided by the Supreme Court; nor do I deny that such decisions must be binding, in any case, upon the parties to a suit, as to the object of that suit, while they are also entitled to very high respect and consideration in all parallel cases by all other departments of the Government. And while it is obviously possible that such decision may be erroneous in any given case, still the evil effect following it, being limited to that particular case, with the chance that it may be overruled, and never become a precedent for other cases, can better be borne than could the evils of a different practice. At the same time, the candid citizen must confess that if the policy of the Government upon vital questions, affecting the whole people, is to be irrevocably fixed by decisions of the Supreme Court, the instant they are made, in ordinary litigation between parties in personal actions, the people will have ceased to be their own rulers, having to that extent practically resigned their government into the hands of that eminent tribunal. Nor is there in this view any assault upon the Court or the Judges. It is a duty from which they may not shrink to decide cases properly brought before them, and it is no fault of theirs if others seek to turn their decisions to political purposes.

One section of our country believes slavery is *right*, and ought to be extended, while the other believes it is *wrong*, and ought not to be extended. This is the only substantial dispute. The fugitive slave clause of the Constitution, and the law for the suppression of the foreign slave trade, are each as well enforced, perhaps, as any law can ever be in a community where the moral sense of the people imperfectly supports the law itself. The great body of the people abide by the dry legal obligation in both cases, and a few break over in each. This, I think, cannot be perfectly cured; and it would be worse in both cases *after* the separation of the sections than before. The foreign slave trade, now imperfectly suppressed, would be ultimately revived without restriction in one section; while fugitive slaves, now only partially surrendered, would not be surrendered at all, by the other.

Physically speaking, we cannot separate. We cannot remove our respective sections from each other, nor build an impassable wall between them. A husband and wife may be divorced, and go out of the presence and beyond the reach of each other; but the different parts of our country cannot do this. They cannot but remain face to face; and intercourse, either amicable or hostile, must continue between them. Is it possible, then, to make that intercourse more advantageous or more satisfactory *after* separation than *before?* Can aliens make treaties easier than friends can make laws? Can treaties be more faithfully enforced between aliens than laws can among friends? Suppose you go to war, you cannot fight always; and when, after much loss on both sides, and no gain on either, you cease fighting, the identical old questions, as to terms of intercourse, are again upon you.

This country, with its institutions, belongs to the people who inhabit it. Whenever they shall grow weary of the existing Government they can exercise their *constitutional* right of amending it, or their *revolutionary* right to dismember or overthrow it. I cannot be ignorant of the fact that many worthy and patriotic citizens are desirous of having the National Constitution amended. While I make no recommendation of amendments, I fully recognize the rightful authority of the people over the whole subject, to be exercised in either of the modes prescribed in the instrument itself; and I should, under existing circumstances, favor rather than oppose a fair opportunity being afforded the people to act upon it. I will venture to add that to me the convention mode seems preferable, in that it allows amendments to originate with the people themselves, instead of only permitting them to take or reject propositions originated by others, not especially chosen for the purpose, and which might not be precisely such as they would wish to either accept or refuse. I understand a proposed amendment to the Constitution—which amendment, however, I have not seen—has passed Congress, to the effect that the Federal Government shall never interfere with the domestic institutions of the States, including that of persons held to service. To avoid misconstruction of what I have said, I depart from my purpose not to speak of particular amendments so far as to say that, holding such a provision to now be implied constitutional law, I have no objection to its being made express and irrevocable.

The Chief Magistrate derives all his authority from the people, and they have conferred none upon him to fix terms for the separation of the States. The people themselves can do this also if they choose; but the Executive, as such, has nothing to do with it. His duty is to administer the present Government, as it came to his hands, and to transmit it, unimpaired by him, to his successor.

Why should there not be a patient confidence in the ultimate justice of the people? Is there any better or equal hope in the world? In our present differences is either party without faith of being in the right? If the Almighty Ruler of Nations, with his eternal truth and justice, be on your side of the North, or on yours of the South, that truth and that justice will surely prevail by the judgment of this great tribunal of the American people.

By the frame of the Government under which we live, this same people have wisely given their public servants but little power for mischief; and have, with equal wisdom, provided for the return of that little to their own hands at very short intervals. While the people retain their virtue and vigilance, no Administration, by any extreme of wickedness or folly, can very seriously injure the Government in the short space of four years.

My countrymen, one and all, think calmly and *well* upon this whole subject. Nothing valuable can be lost by taking time. If there be an object to *hurry* any of you, in hot haste, to a step which you would never take *deliberately*, that object will be frustrated by taking time; but no good object can be frustrated by it. Such of you as are now dissatisfied, still have the old Constitution unimpaired, and, on the sensitive point, the laws of your own framing under it; while the new Administration will have no immediate power, if it would, to change either. If it were admitted that you who are dissatisfied hold the right side in the dispute, there still is no single good reason for precipitate action. Intelligence, patriotism, christianity, and a firm reliance on Him who has never yet forsaken this favored land, are still competent to adjust, in the best way, all our present difficulty.

In *your* hands, my dissatisfied fellow-countrymen, and not in *mine*, is the momentous issue of civil war. The Government will not assail *you*. You can have no conflict without being yourselves the aggressors. *You* have no oath registered in

Ex. Doc. 1——2

Heaven to destroy the Government, while *I* shall have the most solemn one to " preserve, protect, and defend it.''

I am loth to close. We are not enemies, but friends. We must not be enemies. Though passion may have strained, it must not break our bonds of affection. The mystic chords of memory, stretching from every battle-field and patriot grave to every living heart and hearth-stone, all over this broad land, will yet swell the chorus of the Union, when again touched, as surely they will be, by the better angels of our nature.

DEDICATORY ADDRESS

OF

PRESIDENT LINCOLN.

———◆———

FOURSCORE and seven years ago our fathers brought forth upon this continent a new nation, conceived in Liberty, and dedicated to the proposition that all men are created equal.

Now we are engaged in a great civil war, testing whether that nation, or any nation so conceived and so dedicated, can long endure. We are met on a great battle-field of that war. We are met to dedicate a portion of it as the final resting-place of those who here gave their lives that that nation might live. It is altogether fitting and proper that we should do this.

But in a larger sense we cannot dedicate, we cannot consecrate, we cannot hallow this ground. The brave men, living and dead, who struggled here, have consecrated it far above our power to add or detract. The world will little note nor long remember what we say here, but it can never forget what they did here. It is for us, the living, rather to be dedicated here to the unfinished work that they have thus far so nobly carried on. It is rather for us to be here dedicated to the great task remaining before us, — that from these honored dead we take increased devotion to the cause for which they here gave the last full measure of devotion, — that we here highly resolve that the dead shall not have died in vain, that the nation shall, under God, have a new birth of freedom, and that the government of the people, by the people, and for the people, shall not perish from the earth.

INAUGURAL ADDRESS.

MARCH 4, 1865.

FELLOW-COUNTRYMEN: At this second appearing to take the oath of the presidential office, there is less occasion for an extended address than there was at the first. Then, a statement, somewhat in detail, of a course to be pursued, seemed fitting and proper. Now, at the expiration of four years, during which public declarations have been constantly called forth on every point and phase of the great contest which still absorbs the attention and engrosses the energies of the nation, little that is new could be presented. The progress of our arms, upon which all else chiefly depends, is as well known to the public as to myself; and it is, I trust, reasonably satisfactory and encouraging to all. With high hope for the future, no prediction in regard to it is ventured.

On the occasion corresponding to this four years ago, all thoughts were anxiously directed to an impending civil war. All dreaded it—all sought to avert it. While the inaugural address was being delivered from this place, devoted altogether to *saving* the Union without war, insurgent agents were in the city seeking to *destroy* it without war—seeking to dissolve the Union, and divide effects, by negotiation.

INAUGURAL ADDRESS.

Both parties deprecated war; but one of them would *make* war rather than let the nation survive; and the other would *accept* war rather than let it perish. And the war came.

One-eighth of the whole population were colored slaves, not distributed generally over the Union, but localized in the southern part of it. These slaves constituted a peculiar and powerful interest. All knew that this interest was, somehow, the cause of the war. To strengthen, perpetuate and extend this interest was the object for which the insurgents would rend the Union, even by war; while the government claimed no right to do more than to restrict the territorial enlargement of it. Neither party expected for the war the magnitude or the duration which it has already attained. Neither anticipated that the *cause* of the conflict might cease with, or even before, the conflict itself should cease. Each looked for an easier triumph, and a result less fundamental and astounding. Both read the same Bible, and pray to the same God; and each invokes His aid against the other. It may seem strange that any men should dare to ask a just God's assistance in wringing their bread from the sweat of other men's faces; but let us judge not, that we be not judged. The prayers of both could not be answered—that of neither has been answered fully. The Almighty has His own purposes. "Woe unto the world because of offences! for it must needs be that offences come; but woe to that man by whom the offence cometh." If we shall suppose that American slavery is one of those offences which, in the providence of God, must needs come, but which, having continued through His appointed time,

INAUGURAL ADDRESS.

He now wills to remove, and that He gives to both north and south this terrible war, as the woe due to those by whom the offence came, shall we discern therein any departure from those divine attributes which the believers in a living God always ascribe to Him? Fondly do we hope —fervently do we pray—that this mighty scourge of war may speedily pass away. Yet, if God wills that it continue until all the wealth piled by the bondman's two hundred and fifty years of unrequited toil shall be sunk, and until every drop of blood drawn with the lash shall be paid by another drawn with the sword, as was said three thousand years ago, so still it must be said, "The judgments of the Lord are true and righteous altogether."

With malice toward none; with charity for all; with firmness in the right, as God gives us to see the right, let us strive on to finish the work we are in ; to bind up the nation's wounds ; to care for him who shall have borne the battle, and for his widow, and his orphan—to do all which may achieve and cherish a just and a lasting peace among ourselves, and with all nations.

WILLIAM JENNINGS BRYAN

William Jennings Bryan

The Cross of Gold Speech, 1896

WILLIAM JENNINGS BRYAN was as superlative in oratory as Tom Paine was in pamphleteering. The Cross of Gold speech, delivered at Chicago on a stifling July afternoon in 1896 before the Democratic National Convention, not only carried the free silver and pro-income tax planks against the conservative wing of the party but won Bryan the nomination for the presidency. Later it took all the organizing ability and political acumen of a Mark Hanna to beat him in a campaign that aroused the entire nation. In the fullness of time the gold standard has been supplanted not by free silver but by the inflation of the dollar, and millions of Americans pay a graduated income tax. In his insistence that the labor of every man, no matter how humble, contributes to the wealth of the nation, Bryan revived the Jacksonian doctrine of faith in the common man. Because of its eloquent phrases the Cross of Gold address, one of the great political speeches in American history, will long be remembered.

This is a facsimile of one of the earliest, if not the first edition of the Cross of Gold Speech. It is entitled, "Speech delivered by Hon. William J. Bryan, of Nebraska, before the Democratic National Convention, July 9, 1896, . . ." and it was printed in Washington in 1896.

" You shall not press down upon the brow of labor this crown of thorns; you shall not crucify mankind upon a cross of gold."

SPEECH DELIVERED BY

Hon. WILLIAM J. BRYAN,

OF NEBRASKA,

BEFORE THE DEMOCRATIC NATIONAL CONVENTION,

July 9, 1896,

IN CONCLUDING THE DEBATE ON THE ADOPTION OF THE PLATFORM.

MR. CHAIRMAN AND GENTLEMEN OF THE CONVENTION:—I would be presumptious, indeed, to present myself against the distinguished gentlemen to whom you have listened if this was a mere measuring of abilities; but this is not a contest between persons. The humblest citizen in all the land, when clad in the armor of a righteous cause, is stronger than all the hosts of error. I come to speak to you in defense of a cause as holy as the cause of liberty—the cause of humanity.

When this debate is concluded a motion will be made to lay upon the table the resolution offered in commendation of the administration and also the resolution offered in condemnation of the administration. We object to bringing this question down to the level of persons. The individual is but an atom; he is born, he acts, he dies; but principles are eternal; and this has been a contest over a principle.

PRINCIPLES, NOT MEN.

Never before in the history of this country has there been witnessed such a contest as that through which we have just passed. Never before in the history of American politics has a great issue been fought out, as this issue has been, by the voters of a great party. On the 4th of March, 1895, a few Democrats, most of them members of Congress, issued an address to the Democrats of the nation, asserting that the money question was the paramount issue of the hour; declaring that a majority of the Democratic party had the right to control the action of the party on this paramount issue; and concluding with the request that the believers in the free coinage of silver in the Democratic party should organize, take charge of, and control the policy of the Democratic party. Three months later, at Memphis, an organization was perfected, and the silver Democrats went forth openly and courageously proclaiming their belief, and declaring that, if successful, they would crystallize into a platform the declaration which they had made. Then began the conflict. With a zeal approaching the zeal which inspired the crusaders who followed Peter the Hermit, our silver Democrats went forth from victory unto victory until they are now assembled, not to discuss, not to debate, but to enter up the judgment already rendered by the plain people of this country. In this contest brother has been arrayed against brother, father against son. The warmest ties of love, acquaintance, and association have been disregarded; old leaders have been cast aside when they have refused to give expression to the sentiments of those whom they would lead, and new leaders have sprung up to give direction to this cause of truth. Thus has the contest been waged, and we have assembled here under as binding and solemn instructions as were ever imposed upon representatives of the people.

We do not come as individuals. As individuals we might have been glad to compliment the gentleman from New York (Senator Hill), but we know that the people for whom we speak would never be willing to put him in a position where he could thwart the will of the Democratic party. I say it was not a question of persons; it was a question of principle, and it is not with gladness, my friends, that we find ourselves brought into conflict with those who are now arrayed on the other side.

The gentleman who preceded me (ex-Governor Russell) spoke of the State of Massachusetts; let me assure him that not one present in all this convention entertains the least hostility to the people of the State of Massachusetts, but we stand here representing the people who are the equals before the law of the greatest citizens in the State or Massachusetts. When you (turning to the gold delegates) come before us and tell us that we are about to disturb your business interests, we reply that you have disturbed our business interests by your course.

THE REAL BUSINESS MEN.

We say to you that you have made the definition of a business man too limited in its application. The man who is employed for wages is as much a business man as his employer; the atttorney in a country town is as much a business man as the corporation counsel in a great metropolis; the merchant at the cross-roads store is as much a business man as the merchant of New York; the farmer who goes forth in the morning and toils all day—who begins in the spring and toils all summer—and who by the application of brain and muscle to the natural resources of the country creates wealth, is as much a business man as the man who goes upon the board of trade and bets upon the price of grain; the miners who go down a thousand feet into the earth, or climb two thousand feet upon the cliffs, and bring forth from their hiding places the precious metals to be poured into the channels of trade are as much business men as the few financial magnates who, in a back room, corner the money of the world. We come to speak for this broader class of business men.

Ah, my frends, we say not one word against those who live upon the Atlantic coast, but the hardy pioneers who have braved all the dangers of the wilderness, who have made the desert to blossom as the rose—the pioneers away out there (pointing to the West), who rear their children near to Nature's heart, where they can mingle their voices with the voices of the birds—out there where they have erected school houses for the education of their young, churches where they praise their Creator, and cemeteries where rest the ashes of their dead—these people, we say, are as deserving of the consideration of our party as any people in this country. It is for these that we speak. We do not come as aggressors. Our war is not a war of conquest; we are fighting in the defense of our homes, our families, and posterity. We have petitioned, and our petitions have been scorned; we have entreated, and our entreaties have been disregarded; we have begged, and they have mocked when our calamity came. We beg no longer; we entreat no more; we petition no more. We defy them.

The gentleman from Wisconsin has said that he fears a Robespierre. My friends, in this land of the free you need not fear that a tyrant will spring up from among the people. What we need is an Andrew Jackson to stand, as Jackson stood, against the encroachments of organized wealth.

MUST MEET NEW CONDITIONS.

They tell us that this platform was made to catch votes. We reply to them that changing conditions make new issues; that the principles upon which Democracy rests are as everlasting as the hills, but that they must be applied to new conditions as they arise. Conditions have arisen, and we are here to meet those conditions. They tell us that the income tax ought not to be brought in here; that it is a new idea. They criticise us for our criticism of the Supreme Court of the United States. My friends, we have not criticised; we have simply called attention to what you already know. If you want criticisms, read the dissenting opinions of the court. There you will find criticisms. They say that we passed an unconstitutional law; we deny it. The income tax law was not unconstitutional when it was passed; it was not unconstitutional when it went before the Supreme Court for the first time; it did not become unconstitutional until one of the judges changed his mind, and we cannot be expected to know when a judge will change his mind. The income tax is just. It simply intends to put the burdens of government justly upon the backs of the people. I am in favor of an income tax. When I find a man who is not willing to bear his share of the burdens of the government which protects him, I find him a man who is unworthy to enjoy the blessings of a government like ours.

AGAINST A NATIONAL BANK CURRENCY.

They say that they are opposing national bank currency; it is true. If you will read what Thomas Benton said, you will find he said that, in searching history, he could find but one parallel to Andrew Jackson; that was Cicero who destroyed the conspiracy of Cataline and saved Rome. Benton said that Cicero only did for Rome what Jackson did for us when he destroyed the bank conspiracy and saved America. We say in our platform that we believe that the right to coin and issue money is a function of government. We belive it. We believe that it is a part of sovereignty, and can no more with safety be delegated to private individuals than we could afford to delegate to private individuals the power to make penal statutes or levy taxes. Mr. Jefferson, who was once regarded as good Democratic authority, seems to have differed in opinion from the gentleman who has addressed us on the part of the minority. Those who are opposed to this proposition tell us that the issue of paper money is a function of the bank, and that the Government ought to go out of the banking business. I stand with Jefferson rather than with them, and tell them, as he did, that the issue of money is a function of Government, and that the banks ought to go out of the governing business.

They complain about the plank which declares against life tenure in office. They have tried to strain it to mean that which it does not mean. What we oppose by that plank is the life tenure which is being built up in Washington, and which excludes from participation in official benefits the humbler members of society.

THE MINORITY AMENDMENTS.

Let me call your attention to two or three important things The gentleman from New York says that he will propose an amendment to the platform providing that the proposed change in our monetary system shall not affect contracts already made. Let me remind you that there is no intention of affecting those contracts which according to present laws are made payable in gold, but if he means to say that we cannot change our monetary system without protecting those who have loaned money before the change was made, I desire to ask him where, in law, or in morals, he can find justification for not protecting the debtors when the act of 1873 was passed, if he now insists that we must protect the creditors.

He says he will also propose an amendment which will provide for the suspension of free coinage if we fail to maintain the parity within a year. We reply that when we advocate a policy which we believe will be successful, we are not compelled to raise a doubt as to our own sincerity by suggesting what we shall do if we fail. I ask him, if he would apply his logic to us, why he does not apply it to himself. He says he wants this country to try to secure an international agreement. Why does he not tell us what he is going to do if he fails to secure an international agreement? There is more reason for him to do that than there is for us to provide against the failure to maintain a parity. Our opponents have tried for twenty years to secure an international agreement, and those are waiting for it most patiently who do not want it at all.

THE PARAMOUNT ISSUE.

And now, my friends, let me come to the paramount issue. If they ask us why it is that we say more on the money question than we say upon the tariff question, I reply that, if protection has slain its thousands, the gold standard has slain its tens of thousands. If they ask us why we do not embody in our platform all the things that we believe in, we reply that when we have restored the money of the Constitution all other necessary reforms will be possible; but that until this is done there is no other reform that can be accomplished.

Why is it that within three months such a change has come over the country? Three months ago, when it was confidently asserted that those who believe in the gold standard would frame our platform and nominate our candidates, even the advocates of the gold standard did not think that we could elect a president. And they had good reason for their doubt, because there is scarcely a State here to-day asking for the gold standard which is not in the absolute control of the Republican party. But note the change. Mr. McKinley was nominated at St. Louis upon a platform which declared for the maintenance of the gold standard until it can be changed into bimetallism by international agreement. Mr. McKinley was the most popular man among the Republicans, and three months ago everybody in the Republican party prophesied his election. How is it to-day? Why, the man who was once pleased to think that he looked like Napoleon—that man shudders to-day when he remembers that he was nominated on the anniversary of the battle of Waterloo. Not only that, but, as he listens, he can hear, with ever-increasing distinctness, the sound of the waves as they beat upon the lonely shores of St. Helena.

Why this change? Ah, my friends, is not the reason for the change evident to any one who will look at the matter? No private character, however pure, no personal popularity, however great, can protect from the avenging wrath of an indignant people a man who will declare that he is in favor of fastening the gold standard upon this country or who is willing to surrender the right of self government and place the legislative control of our affairs in the hands of foreign potentates and powers.

CONFIDENT OF SUCCESS.

We go forth confident that we shall win. Why? Because upon the paramount issue of this campaign there is not a spot of ground upon which the enemy will dare to challenge battle. If they tell us that the gold standard is a good thing, we shall point to their platform and tell them that their platform pledges the party to get rid of the gold standard and substitute bimetallism. If the gold standard is a good thing, why try to get rid of it? I call your attention to the fact that some of the very people who are in this convention to-day and who tell us that we ought to declare in favor of international bimetallism—thereby declaring that the gold standard is wrong and that the principle of bimetallism is better—these very people four months ago were open and avowed advocates of the gold standard, and were then telling us that we could not legislate two metals together, even with the aid of all the world. If the gold standard is a good thing, we ought to declare in favor of its retention and not in favor of abandoning it; and if the gold standard is a bad thing, why should we wait until other nations are willing to help us to let go? Here is the line of battle, and we care not upon which issue they force the fight; we are prepared to meet them on either issue or on both. If they tell us that the gold standard is the standard of civilization, we reply to them that this, the most enlightened of all the nations of the earth, has never declared for a gold standard and that both the great parties this year are declaring against it. If the gold standard is the standard of civilization why, my friends, should we not have it? If they come to meet us on that issue we can present the history of our nation. More than that; we can tell them that they will search the pages of history in vain to find a single instance where the common people of any land have ever declared themselves in favor of the gold standard. They can find where the holders of fixed investments have declared for a gold standard, but not where the masses have.

CARLISLE DEFINES THE ISSUE.

Mr. Carlisle said, in 1878, that this was a struggle between "the idle holders of idle capital" and "the struggling masses, who produce the wealth and pay the taxes of the country," and, my friends, the question we are to decide is: Upon which side will the Democratic party fight: upon the side of the "idle holders of idle capital" or upon the side of the "struggling masses?" That is the question which the party must answer first, and then it must be answered by each individual hereafter. The sympathies of the Democratic party, as shown by the platform, are on the side of the struggling masses who have ever been the foundation of the Democratic party. There are two ideas of government. There are those who believe that, if you will only legislate to make the well-to-do prosperous, their prosperity will leak through on those below. The Democratic idea, however, has been that if you legislate to make the masses prosperous, their prosperity will find its way up through every class which rests upon them.

You come to us and tell us that the great cities are in favor of the gold standard; we reply that the great cities rest upon our broad and fertile prairies. Burn down your cities and leave our farms and your cities will spring up again as if by magic; but destroy our farms and the grass will grow in the streets of every city in the country.

A NEW DECLARATION OF INDEPENDENCE.

My friends, we declare that this nation is able to legislate for its own people on every question, without waiting for the aid or consent of any other nation on earth; and upon that issue we expect to carry every State in the Union. I shall not slander the inhabitants of the fair State of Massachusetts nor the inhabitants of the State of New York by saying that, when they are confronted with the proposition, they will declare that this nation is not able to attend to its own business. It is the issue of 1776 over again. Our ancestors, when but three millions in number, had the courage to declare their political independence of every other nation; shall we, their descendants, when we have grown to seventy millions, declare that we are less independent than our forefathers? No, my friends, that will never be the verdict of our people. Therefore, we care not upon what lines the battle is fought. If they say bimetallism is good, but that we cannot have it until other nations help us, we reply that, instead of having a gold standard because England has, we will restore bimetallism, and then let England have bimetallism because the United States has it. If they dare to come out into the open field and defend the gold standard as a good thing, we will fight them to the uttermost. Having behind us the producing masses of this nation and the world, supported by the commercial interests, the laboring interests, and the toilers everywhere, we will answer their demand for a gold standard by saying to them: "You shall not press down upon the brow of labor this crown of thorns; you shall not crucify mankind upon a cross of gold."

John F. Sheiry, Printer, 623 D Street, N. W., Washington, D. C.

THEODORE ROOSEVELT

Theodore Roosevelt

>>>>>>>>>>>>>>>>>>>>>>>>>>>>>><<<<<<<<<<<<<<<<<<<<<<<<<<<<

Foreign Affairs, 1904, and the Monroe Doctrine, 1905

W ITH THEODORE ROOSEVELT, the United States began to take a vital interest in problems of peace and war throughout the world. In his Message of 1904 President Roosevelt gave a clear exposition of the new role of the United States in world affairs and of her especial interest in the Western Hemisphere. In his Message of 1905, he enunciated what became known as the Roosevelt Corollary to the Monroe Doctrine. He indicated in no uncertain terms that the European powers must look first to the United States for the discharge of financial obligations by defaulting Latin American states. President Roosevelt had ample reason for suspecting that certain European governments had ambitions in Latin America. But his declaration that the United States would exercise "an international police power" in Latin America was soon resented there as "Yankee Imperialism." It was not until 1930, under Secretary of State Stimson, that the Monroe Doctrine was redefined, thus paving the way for the "Good Neighbor" policy of the present. These passages from the presidential messages reveal President Roosevelt's vigorous and forward-looking thinking upon international order. His maxim, borrowed from the range, was, "Never draw unless you mean to shoot."

These excerpts are facsimiles of the official messages to Congress. The first selection is contained in the "Papers relating to the Foreign Relations of the United States, with the Annual Message of the President, transmitted to Congress December 6, 1904" (Washington, Government Printing Office, 1905), and the second is contained in the "Message of the President of the United States communicated to the two houses of Congress at the beginning of the First Session of the Fifty-ninth Congress" (Washington, Government Printing Office, 1906).

THEODORE ROOSEVELT
ON FOREIGN AFFAIRS
from the Message to Congress, December 6, 1904

. . . .

In treating of our foreign policy and of the attitude that this great Nation should assume in the world at large, it is absolutely necessary to consider the Army and the Navy, and the Congress, through which the thought of the Nation finds its **Foreign policy.** expression, should keep ever vividly in mind the fundamental fact that it is impossible to treat our foreign policy, whether this policy takes shape in the effort to secure justice for others or justice for ourselves, save as conditioned upon the attitude we are willing to take toward our Army, and especially toward our Navy. It is not merely unwise, it is contemptible, for a nation, as for an individual, to use high-sounding language to proclaim its purposes, or to take positions which are ridiculous if unsupported by potential force, and then to refuse to provide this force. If there is no intention of providing and of keeping the force necessary to back up a strong attitude, then it is far better not to assume such an attitude.

The steady aim of this Nation, as of all enlightened nations, should be to strive to bring ever nearer the day when there shall prevail throughout the world the peace of justice. There are kinds of peace which are highly undesirable, which are in the long run as destructive as any war. Tyrants and oppressors have many times made a wilderness and called it peace. Many times peoples who were slothful or timid or shortsighted, who had been enervated by ease or by luxury, or misled by false teachings, have shrunk in unmanly fashion from doing duty that was stern and that needed self-sacrifice, and have sought to hide from their own minds their shortcomings, their ignoble motives, by calling them love of peace. The peace of tyrannous terror, the peace of craven weakness, the peace of injustice, all these should be shunned as we shun unrighteous war. The goal to set before us as a nation, the goal which should be set before all mankind, is the attainment of the peace of justice, of the peace which comes when each nation is not merely safe-guarded in its own rights, but scrupulously recognizes and performs its duty toward others.

Generally peace tells for righteousness; but if there is conflict between the two, then our fealty is due first to the cause of righteousness. Unrighteous wars are common, and unrighteous peace is rare; but both should be shunned. The right of freedom and the responsibility for the exercise of that right can not be divorced. One of our great poets has well and finely said that freedom is not a gift that tarries long in the hands of cowards. Neither does it tarry long in the hands of those too slothful, too dishonest, or too unintelligent to exercise it. The eternal vigilance which is the price of liberty must be exercised, sometimes to guard against outside foes; although of course far more often to guard against our own selfish or thoughtless shortcomings.

If these self-evident truths are kept before us, and only if they are so kept before us, we shall have a clear idea of what our foreign policy in its larger aspects should be. It is our duty to remember that a nation has no more right to do injustice to another nation, strong or weak, than an individual has to do injustice to another individual; that the same moral law applies in one case as in the other. But we must also remember that it is as much the duty of the Nation to guard its own rights and its own interests as it is the duty of the individual so to do. Within the Nation the individual has now delegated this right to the State, that is, to the representative of all the individuals, and it is a maxim of the law that for every wrong there is a remedy. But in international law we have not advanced by any means as far as we have advanced in municipal law. There is as yet no judicial way of enforcing a right in international law. When one nation wrongs another or wrongs many others, there is no tribunal before which the wrongdoer can be brought. Either it is necessary supinely to acquiesce in the wrong, and thus put a premium upon brutality and aggression, or else it is necessary for the aggrieved nation valiantly to stand up for its rights. Until some method is devised by which there shall be a degree of international control over offending nations, it would be a wicked thing for the most civilized powers, for those with most sense of international obligations and with keenest and most generous appreciation of the difference between right and wrong, to disarm. If the great civilized nations of the present day should completely disarm, the result would mean an immediate recrudescence of barbarism in one form or another. Under any circumstances a sufficient armament would have to be kept up to serve the purposes of international police; and until international cohesion and the sense of international duties and rights are far more advanced than at present, a nation desirous both of securing respect for itself and of doing good to others must have a force adequate for the work which it feels is allotted to it as its part of the general world duty. Therefore it follows that a self-respecting, just, and far-seeing nation should on the one hand endeavor by every means to aid in the development of the various movements which tend to provide substitutes for war, which tend to render nations in their actions toward one another, and indeed toward their own peoples, more responsive to the general sentiment of humane and civilized mankind; and on the other hand that it should keep prepared, while scrupulously avoiding wrongdoing itself, to repel any wrong, and in exceptional cases to take action which in a more advanced stage of international relations would come under the head of the exercise of the international police. A great free people owes it to itself and to all mankind not to sink into helplessness before the powers of evil.

We are in every way endeavoring to help on, with cordial good will, every movement which will tend to bring us into more friendly relations with the rest of mankind. In pursuance of this policy I shall shortly lay before the Senate treaties of arbitration with all powers which are willing to enter into these treaties with us. It is not possible at this period of the world's development to agree to arbitrate all matters, but there are many matters of possible difference between us and other nations which can be thus arbitrated. Furthermore, at the request of the Interparliamentary Union, an eminent body composed of practical statesmen from all countries, I have asked the Powers to join with this Government in a second Hague conference, at which it is hoped that the work already so happily begun at The Hague may be carried some steps further toward completion. This carries out the desire expressed by the first Hague conference itself.

Arbitration treaties.

Second Hague conference.

It is not true that the United States feels any land hunger or entertains any projects as regards the other nations of the Western Hemisphere save such as are for their welfare. All that this country desires is to see the neighboring countries stable, orderly, and prosperous. Any country whose people conduct themselves well can count upon our hearty friendship. If a nation shows that it knows how to act with reasonable efficiency and decency in social and political matters, if it keeps order and pays its obligations, it need fear no interference from the United States. Chronic wrong-

Policy toward other nations of Western Hemisphere.

doing, or an impotence which results in a general loosening of the ties of civilized society, may in America, as elsewhere, ultimately require intervention by some civilized nation, and in the Western Hemisphere the adherence of the United States to the Monroe Doctrine may force the United States, however reluctantly, in flagrant cases of such wrongdoing or impotence, to the exercise of an international police power. If every country washed by the Caribbean Sea would show the progress in stable and just civilization which with the aid of the Platt amendment Cuba has shown since our troops left the island, and which so many of the republics in both Americas are constantly and brilliantly showing, all question of interference by this Nation with their affairs would be at an end. Our interests and those of our southern neighbors are in reality identical. They have great natural riches, and if within their borders the reign of law and justice obtains, prosperity is sure to come to them. While they thus obey the primary laws of civilized society they may rest assured that they will be treated by us in a spirit of cordial and helpful sympathy. We would interfere with them only in the last resort, and then only if it became evident that their inability or unwillingness to do justice at home and abroad had violated the rights of the United States or had invited foreign aggression to the detriment of the entire body of American nations. It is a mere truism to say that every nation, whether in America or anywhere else, which desires to maintain its freedom, its independence, must ultimately realize that the right of such independence can not be separated from the responsibility of making good use of it.

In asserting the Monroe Doctrine, in taking such steps as we have taken in regard to Cuba, Venezuela, and Panama, and in endeavoring to circumscribe the theater of war in the Far East, and to secure the open door in China, we have acted in our own interest as well as in the interest of humanity at large. There are, however, cases in which, while our own interests are not greatly involved, strong appeal is made to our sympathies. Ordinarily it is very much wiser and more useful for us to concern ourselves with striving for our own moral and material betterment here at home than to concern ourselves with trying to better the condition of things in other nations. We have plenty of sins of our own to war against, and under ordinary circumstances we can do more for the general uplifting of humanity by striving with heart and soul to put a stop to civic corruption, to brutal lawlessness and violent race prejudices here at home than by passing resolutions about wrongdoing elsewhere. Nevertheless there are occasional crimes committed on so vast a scale and of such peculiar horror as to make us doubt whether it is not our manifest duty to endeavor at least to show our disapproval of the deed and our sympathy with those who have suffered by it. The cases must be extreme in which such a course is justifiable. There must be no effort made to remove the mote from our brother's eye if we refuse to remove the beam from our own. But in extreme cases action may be justifiable and proper. What form the action shall take must depend upon the circumstances of the case; that is, upon the degree of the atrocity and upon our power to remedy it. The cases in which we could interfere by force of arms as we interfered to put a stop to intolerable conditions in Cuba are necessarily very few. Yet it is not to be expected that a people like ours, which in spite of certain very obvious shortcomings, nevertheless as a whole shows by its consistent practice its belief in the principles of civil and religious liberty and of orderly freedom, a people among whom even the worst crime, like the crime of lynching, is never more than sporadic, so that individuals and not classes are molested in their fundamental rights—it is inevitable that such a nation should desire eagerly to give expression to its horror on an occasion like that of the massacre of the Jews in Kishenef, or when it witnesses such systematic and long-extended cruelty and oppression as the cruelty and oppression of which the Armenians have been the victims, and which have won for them the indignant pity of the civilized world.

.   .   .   .

THEODORE ROOSEVELT
COROLLARY TO THE MONROE DOCTRINE
from the Message to Congress, December 5, 1905

. . . .

One of the most effective instruments for peace is the Monroe Doctrine as it has been and is being gradually developed by this Nation and accepted by other nations. No other policy could have been as efficient in promoting peace in the Western Hemisphere and in giving to each nation thereon the chance to develop along its own lines. If we had refused to apply the Doctrine to changing conditions it would now be completely outworn, would not meet any of the needs of the present day, and indeed would probably by this time have sunk into complete oblivion. It is useful at home, and is meeting with recognition abroad because we have adapted our application of it to meet the growing and changing needs of the Hemisphere. When we announce a policy, such as the Monroe Doctrine, we thereby commit ourselves to the consequences of the policy, and those consequences from time to time alter. It is out of the question to claim a right and yet shirk the responsibility for its exercise. Not only we, but all American Republics who are benefited by the existence of the Doctrine, must recognize the obligations each nation is under as regards foreign peoples no less than its duty to insist upon its own rights.

Monroe Doctrine.

That our rights and interests are deeply concerned in the maintenance of the Doctrine is so clear as hardly to need argument. This is especially true in view of the construction of the Panama Canal. As a mere matter of self-defense we must exercise a close watch over the approaches to this canal; and this means that we must be thoroughly alive to our interests in the Caribbean Sea.

There are certain essential points which must never be forgotten as regards the Monroe Doctrine. In the first place we must as a nation make it evident that we do not intend to treat it in any shape or way as an excuse for aggrandizement on our part at the expense of the republics to the south. We must recognize the fact that in some South American countries there has been much suspicion lest we should interpret the Monroe Doctrine as in some way inimical to their interests, and we must try to convince all the other nations of this continent once and for all that no just and orderly government has anything to fear from us. There are certain republics to the south of us which have already reached such a point of stability, order, and prosperity that they themselves, though as yet hardly consciously, are among the guarantors of this Doctrine. These republics we now meet not only on a basis of entire equality, but in a spirit of frank and respectful friendship, which we hope is mutual. If all of the republics to the south of us will only grow as those to which I allude have already grown, all need for us to be the especial champions of the Doctrine will disappear, for no stable and growing American Republic wishes to see some great non-American military power acquire territory in its neighborhood. All that this country desires is that the other republics on this Continent shall be happy and prosperous; and they can not be happy and prosperous unless they maintain order within their boundaries and behave with a just regard for their obligations toward outsiders. It must be understood that under no circumstances will the United States use the Monroe Doctrine as a cloak for territorial aggression. We desire peace with all the world, but perhaps most of all with the other peoples of the American Continent. There are of course limits to the wrongs which any self-respecting nation can endure. It is always possible that wrong actions toward this Nation, or toward citizens of this Nation, in some State unable to keep order among its own people, unable to secure justice from outsiders, and unwilling to do justice to those outsiders who treat it well, may result in our having to take action to protect our rights; but such action will not be taken with a view to territorial aggression, and it will be taken at all only with extreme reluctance and when it has become evident that every other resource has been exhausted.

Moreover, we must make it evident that we do not intend to permit the Monroe Doctrine to be used by any nation on this Continent as a shield to protect it from the consequences of its own misdeeds against foreign nations. If a republic to the south of us commits a tort against a foreign nation, such as an outrage against a citizen of that nation, then the Monroe Doctrine does not force us to interfere to prevent punishment of the tort, save to see that the punishment does not assume the form of territorial occupation in any shape. The case is more difficult when it refers to a contractual obligation. Our own Government has always refused to enforce such contractual obligations on behalf of its citizens by an appeal to arms. It is much to be wished that all foreign governments would take the same view. But they do not; and in consequence we are liable at any time to be brought face to face with disagreeable alternatives. On the one hand, this country would certainly decline to go to war to prevent a foreign government from collecting a just debt; on the other hand, it is very inadvisable to permit any foreign power to take possession, even temporarily, of the custom-houses of an American Republic in order to enforce the payment of its obligations; for such temporary occupation might turn into a permanent occupation. The only escape from these alternatives may at any time be that we must ourselves undertake to bring about some arrangement by which so much as possible of a just obligation shall be paid. It is far better that this country should put through such an arrangement, rather than allow any foreign country to undertake it. To do so insures the defaulting republic from having to pay debts of an improper character under duress, while it also insures honest creditors of the republic from being passed by in the interest of dishonest or grasping creditors. Moreover, for the United States to take such a position offers the only possible way of insuring us against a clash with some foreign power. The position is, therefore, in the interest of peace as well as in the interest of justice. It is of benefit to our people; it is of benefit to foreign peoples; and most of all it is really of benefit to the people of the country concerned.

This brings me to what should be one of the fundamental objects of the Monroe Doctrine. We must ourselves in good faith try to help upward toward peace and order those of our sister republics which need such help. Just as there has been a gradual growth of the ethical element in the relations of one individual to another, so we are, even though slowly, more and more coming to recognize the duty of bearing one another's burdens, not only as among individuals, but also as among nations.

Santo Domingo, in her turn, has now made an appeal to us to help her, and not only every principle of wisdom but every generous instinct within us bids us respond to the appeal. It is not of the slightest consequence whether we grant the aid needed by Santo Domingo as an incident to the wise development of the Monroe Doctrine, or because we regard the case of Santo Domingo as standing wholly by itself, and to be treated as such, and not on general principles or with any reference to the Monroe Doctrine. The important point is to give the needed aid, and the case is certainly sufficiently peculiar to deserve to be judged purely on its own merits. The conditions in Santo Domingo have for a number of years grown from bad to worse until a year ago all society was on the verge

Santo Domingo.

of dissolution. Fortunately, just at this time a ruler sprang up in Santo Domingo, who, with his colleagues, saw the dangers threatening their country and appealed to the friendship of the only great and powerful neighbor who possessed the power, and as they hoped also the will to help them. There was imminent danger of foreign intervention. The previous rulers of Santo Domingo had recklessly incurred debts, and owing to her internal disorders she had ceased to be able to provide means of paying the debts. The patience of her foreign creditors had become exhausted, and at least two foreign nations were on the point of intervention, and were only prevented from intervening by the unofficial assurance of this Government that it would itself strive to help Santo Domingo in her hour of need. In the case of one of these nations, only the actual opening of negotiations to this end by our Government prevented the seizure of territory in Santo Domingo by a European power. Of the debts incurred some were just, while some were not of a character which really renders it obligatory on, or proper for, Santo Domingo to pay them in full. But she could not pay any of them unless some stability was assured her Government and people.

Accordingly the Executive Department of our Government negotiated a treaty under which we are to try to help the Dominican people to straighten out their finances. This treaty is pending before the Senate. In the meantime a temporary arrangement has been made which will last until the Senate has had time to take action upon the treaty. Under this arrangement the Dominican Government has appointed Americans to all the important positions in the customs service, and they are seeing to the honest collection of the revenues, turning over 45 per cent to the Government for running expenses and putting the other 55 per cent into a safe depositary for equitable division in case the treaty shall be ratified, among the various creditors, whether European or American.

The custom-houses offer well-nigh the only sources of revenue in Santo Domingo, and the different revolutions usually have as their real aim the obtaining possession of these custom-houses. The mere fact that the collectors of customs are Americans, that they are performing their duties with efficiency and honesty, and that the treaty is pending in the Senate, gives a certain moral power to the Government of Santo Domingo which it has not had before. This has completely discouraged all revolutionary movement, while it has already produced such an increase in the revenues that the Government is actually getting more from the 45 per cent that the

American collectors turn over to it than it got formerly when it took the entire revenue. It is enabling the poor harassed people of Santo Domingo once more to turn their attention to industry and to be free from the curse of interminable revolutionary disturbance. It offers to all bona fide creditors, American and European, the only really good chance to obtain that to which they are justly entitled, while it in return gives to Santo Domingo the only opportunity of defense against claims which it ought not to pay, for now if it meets the views of the Senate we shall ourselves thoroughly examine all these claims, whether American or foreign, and see that none that are improper are paid. There is, of course, opposition to the treaty from dishonest creditors, foreign and American, and from the professional revolutionists of the island itself. We have already reason to believe that some of the creditors who do not dare expose their claims to honest scrutiny are endeavoring to stir up sedition in the island and opposition to the treaty. In the meantime I have exercised the authority vested in me by the joint resolution of the Congress to prevent the introduction of arms into the island for revolutionary purposes.

Under the course taken, stability and order and all the benefits of peace are at last coming to Santo Domingo, danger of foreign intervention has been suspended, and there is at last a prospect that all creditors will get justice, no more and no less. If the arrangement is terminated by the failure of the treaty chaos will follow; and if chaos follows, sooner or later this Government may be involved in serious difficulties with foreign governments over the island, or else may be forced itself to intervene in the island in some unpleasant fashion. Under the proposed treaty the independence of the island is scrupulously respected, the danger of violation of the Monroe Doctrine by the intervention of foreign powers vanishes, and the interference of our Government is minimized, so that we shall only act in conjunction with the Santo Domingo authorities to secure the proper administration of the customs, and therefore to secure the payment of just debts and to secure the Dominican Government against demands for unjust debts. The proposed method will give the people of Santo Domingo the same chance to move onward and upward which we have already given to the people of Cuba. It will be doubly to our discredit as a nation if we fail to take advantage of this chance; for it will be of damage to ourselves, and it will be of incalculable damage to Santo Domingo. Every consideration of wise policy, and, above all, every consideration of large generosity, bids us meet the request of Santo Domingo as we are now trying to meet it.

.   .   .   .

WOODROW WILSON

Woodrow Wilson

>>>>>>>>>>>>>>>>>>>>>>>><<<<<<<<<<<<<<<<<<<<<<<<

Presenting the Treaty of Versailles for Ratification, 1919

To ALL but the most cynical, Wilson's address to the Senate on July 10, 1919, is one of the most memorable in American history. That Wilson would fail in his appeal for ratification for the Versailles Treaty and Covenant of the League of Nations was a foregone conclusion. He faced a Republican Senate and a Republican Foreign Relations Committee. Since the Republicans had loyally supported all his war measures, he had erred in calling for a Democratic Congress in the elections of 1918 and he had erred in failing to invite leading Republicans to serve on the American Peace Commission. The debate that followed his address was waged in the press and by the public as well as in the Senate. While amendments were being urged by Senator Lodge and others, Wilson, in September, 1919, took his case to the people in a speaking trip and collapsed at Pueblo, Colorado, before completing it. The Treaty was finally defeated in March, 1920. In July, 1921, a simple joint resolution was passed by both houses of Congress declaring an end to the war with Germany. The United States did not sign the Treaty and did not join the League of Nations. Only President Wilson's courageous plea remains for us to ponder.

This is a facsimile of the official Senate document No. 50, Sixty-sixth Congress (Washington, Government Printing Office, 1919). This copy was kindly lent by the Library of the University of California at Los Angeles.

TREATY OF PEACE WITH GERMANY.

GENTLEMEN OF THE SENATE: The treaty of peace with Germany was signed at Versailles on the twenty-eighth of June. I avail myself of the earliest opportunity to lay the treaty before you for ratification and to inform you with regard to the work of the Conference by which that treaty was formulated.

The treaty constitutes nothing less than a world settlement. It would not be possible for me either to summarize or to construe its manifold provisions in an address which must of necessity be something less than a treatise. My services and all the information I possess will be at your disposal and at the disposal of your Committee on Foreign Relations at any time, either informally or in session, as you may prefer; and I hope that you will not hesitate to make use of them. I shall at this time, prior to your own study of the document, attempt only a general characterization of its scope and purpose.

In one sense, no doubt, there is no need that I should report to you what was attempted and done at Paris. You have been daily cognizant of what was going on there,—of the problems with which the Peace Conference had to deal and of the difficulty of laying down straight lines of settlement anywhere on a field on which the old lines of international relationship, and the new alike, followed so intricate a pattern and were for the most part cut so deep by historical circumstances which dominated action even where it would have been best to ignore or reverse them. The cross currents of politics and of interest must have been evident to you. It would be presuming in me to attempt to explain the questions which arose or the many diverse elements that entered into them. I shall attempt something less ambitious than that and more clearly suggested by my duty to report to the Congress the part it seemed necessary for my colleagues and me to play as the representatives of the Government of the United States.

That part was dictated by the role America had played in the war and by the expectations that had been created in the minds of the peoples with whom we had associated ourselves in that great struggle.

The United States entered the war upon a different footing from every other nation except our associates on this side the sea. We entered it, not because our material interests were directly threatened

or because any special treaty obligations to which we were parties
had been violated, but only because we saw the supremacy, and even
the validity, of right everywhere put in jeopardy and free government likely to be everywhere imperiled by the intolerable aggression
of a power which respected neither right nor obligation and whose
very system of government flouted the rights of the citizen as against
the autocratic authority of his governors. And in the settlements of
the peace we have sought no special reparation for ourselves, but only
the restoration of right and the assurance of liberty everywhere
that the effects of the settlement were to be felt. We entered the
war as the disinterested champions of right and we interested ourselves in the terms of the peace in no other capacity.

The hopes of the nations allied against the central powers were at
a very low ebb when our soldiers began to pour across the sea. There
was everywhere amongst them, except in their stoutest spirits, a
sombre foreboding of disaster. The war ended in November, eight
months ago, but you have only to recall what was feared in midsum-
mer last, four short months before the armistice, to realize what it
was that our timely aid accomplished alike for their morale and their
physical safety. That first, never-to-be-forgotten action at Chateau-
Thierry had already taken place. Our redoutable soldiers and ma-
rines had already closed the gap the enemy had succeeded in opening
for their advance upon Paris,—had already turned the tide of battle
back towards the frontiers of France and begun the rout that was to
save Europe and the world. Thereafter the Germans were to be
always forced back, back, were never to thrust successfully forward
again. And yet there was no confident hope. Anxious men and
women, leading spirits of France, attended the celebration of the
fourth of July last year in Paris out of generous courtesy,—with no
heart for festivity, little zest for hope. But they came away with
something new at their hearts: they have themselves told us so. The
mere sight of our men,—of their vigour, of the confidence that showed
itself in every movement of their stalwart figures and every turn of
their swinging march, in their steady comprehending eyes and easy
discipline, in the indomitable air that added spirit to everything they
did,—made everyone who saw them that memorable day realize that
something had happened that was much more than a mere incident
in the fighting, something very different from the mere arrival of
fresh troops. A great moral force had flung itself into the struggle.
The fine physical force of those spirited men spoke of something more
than bodily vigour. They carried the great ideals of a free people
at their hearts and with that vision were unconquerable. Their very
presence brought reassurance; their fighting made victory certain.

They were recognized as crusaders, and as their thousands swelled
to millions their strength was seen to mean salvation. And they were

fit men to carry such a hope and make good the assurance it forecast. Finer men never went into battle; and their officers were worthy of them. This is not the occasion upon which to utter a eulogy of the armies America sent to France, but perhaps, since I am speaking of their mission, I may speak also of the pride I shared with every American who saw or dealt with them there. They were the sort of men America would wish to be represented by, the sort of men every American would wish to claim as fellowcountrymen and comrades in a great cause. They were terrible in battle, and gentle and helpful out of it, remembering the mothers and the sisters, the wives and the little children at home. They were free men under arms, not forgetting their ideals of duty in the midst of tasks of violence. I am proud to have had the privilege of being associated with them and of calling myself their leader.

But I speak now of what they meant to the men by whose sides they fought and to the people with whom they mingled with such utter simplicity, as friends who asked only to be of service. They were for all the visible embodiment of America. What they did made America and all that she stood for a living reality in the thoughts not only of the people of France but also of tens of millions of men and women throughout all the toiling nations of a world standing everywhere in peril of its freedom and of the loss of everything it held dear, in deadly fear that its bonds were never to be loosed, its hopes forever to be mocked and disappointed.

And the compulsion of what they stood for was upon us who represented America at the peace table. It was our duty to see to it that every decision we took part in contributed, so far as we were able to influence it, to quiet the fears and realize the hopes of the peoples who had been living in that shadow, the nations that had come by our assistance to their freedom. It was our duty to do everything that it was within our power to do to make the triumph of freedom and of right a lasting triumph in the assurance of which men might everywhere live without fear.

Old entanglements of every kind stood in the way,—promises which Governments had made to one another in the days when might and right were confused and the power of the victor was without restraint. Engagements which contemplated any dispositions of territory, any extensions of sovereignty that might seem to be to the interest of those who had the power to insist upon them, had been entered into without thought of what the peoples concerned might wish or profit by; and these could not always be honourably brushed aside. It was not easy to graft the new order of ideas on the old, and some of the fruits of the grafting may, I fear, for a time be bitter. But, with very few exceptions, the men who sat with us at the peace table desired as sincerely as we did to get away from the bad influences, the illegitimate purposes, the demoralizing ambitions, the international counsels and expedients out of which the sinister designs of Germany had sprung as a natural growth.

It had been our privilege to formulate the principles which were accepted as the basis of the peace, but they had been accepted, not because we had come in to hasten and assure the victory and insisted upon them, but because they were readily acceded to as the principles to which honourable and enlightened minds everywhere had been bred. They spoke the conscience of the world as well as the conscience of America, and I am happy to pay my tribute of respect and gratitude to the able, forward-looking men with whom it was my privilege to cooperate for their unfailing spirit of cooperation, their constant effort to accommodate the interests they represented to the principles we were all agreed upon. The difficulties, which were many, lay in the circumstances, not often in the men. Almost without exception the men who led had caught the true and full vision of the problem of peace as an indivisible whole, a problem, not of mere adjustments of interest, but of justice and right action.

The atmosphere in which the Conference worked seemed created, not by the ambitions of strong governments, but by the hopes and aspirations of small nations and of peoples hitherto under bondage to the power that victory had shattered and destroyed. Two great empires had been forced into political bankruptcy, and we were the receivers. Our task was not only to make peace with the central empires and remedy the wrongs their armies had done. The central empires had lived in open violation of many of the very rights for which the war had been fought, dominating alien peoples over whom they had no natural right to rule, enforcing, not obedience, but veritable bondage, exploiting those who were weak for the benefit of those who were masters and overlords only by force of arms. There could be no peace until the whole order of central Europe was set right.

That meant that new nations were to be created,—Poland, Czecho-Slovakia, Hungary itself. No part of ancient Poland had ever in any true sense become a part of Germany, or of Austria, or of Russia. Bohemia was alien in every thought and hope to the monarchy of which she had so long been an artificial part; and the uneasy partnership between Austria and Hungary had been one rather of interest than of kinship or sympathy. The Slavs whom Austria had chosen to force into her empire on the south were kept to their obedience by nothing but fear. Their hearts were with their kinsmen in the Balkans. These were all arrangements of power, not arrangements of natural union or association. It was the imperative task of those who would make peace and make it intelligently to establish a new order which would rest upon the free choice of peoples rather than upon the arbitrary authority of Hapsburgs or Hohenzollerns.

More than that, great populations bound by sympathy and actual kin to Rumania were also linked against their will to the conglomerate Austro-Hungarian monarchy or to other alien sovereignties, and it was part of the task of peace to make a new Rumania as well as a new slavic state clustering about Serbia.

And no natural frontiers could be found to these new fields of adjustment and redemption. It was necessary to look constantly forward to other related tasks. The German colonies were to be disposed of. They had not been governed; they had been exploited merely, without thought of the interest or even the ordinary human rights of their inhabitants.

The Turkish Empire, moreover, had fallen apart, as the Austro-Hungarian had. It had never had any real unity. It had been held together only by pitiless, inhuman force. Its peoples cried aloud for release, for succour from unspeakable distress, for all that the new day of hope seemed at last to bring within its dawn. Peoples hitherto in utter darkness were to be led out into the same light and given at last a helping hand. Undeveloped peoples and peoples ready for recognition but not yet ready to assume the full responsibilities of statehood were to be given adequate guarantees of friendly protection, guidance, and assistance.

And out of the execution of these great enterprises of liberty sprang opportunities to attempt what statesmen had never found the way before to do; an opportunity to throw safeguards about the rights of racial, national, and religious minorities by solemn international covenant; an opportunity to limit and regulate military establishments where they were most likely to be mischievous; an opportunity to effect a complete and systematic internationalization of waterways and railways which were necessary to the free economic life of more than one nation and to clear many of the normal channels of commerce of unfair obstructions of law or of privilege; and the very welcome opportunity to secure for labour the concerted protection of definite international pledges of principle and practice.

These were not tasks which the Conference looked about it to find and went out of its way to perform. They were inseparable from the settlements of peace. They were thrust upon it by circumstances which could not be overlooked. The war had created them. In all quarters of the world old established relationships had been disturbed or broken and affairs were at loose ends, needing to be mended or united again, but could not be made what they were before. They had to be set right by applying some uniform principle of justice or enlightened expediency. And they could not be adjusted by merely prescribing in a treaty what should be done. New states were to be set up which could not hope to live through their first period of weakness without assured support by the great nations that had consented to their creation and won for them their independence. Ill governed colonies could not be put in the hands of governments which were to act as trustees for their people and not as their masters if there was to be no common authority among the nations to which they were to be responsible in the execution of their trust. Future international conventions with regard to the control of waterways, with regard to illicit traffic of many kinds, in arms or in deadly drugs, or with regard to the adjustment of many varying international administrative arrangements could not be assured if the treaty were to provide no permanent common international agency, if its execution in such matters was to be left to the slow and uncertain processes of cooperation by ordinary methods of negotiation. If the Peace Conference itself was to be the end of cooperative authority and common counsel among the governments to which the world was looking to enforce justice and give pledges of an enduring settlement, regions like the Saar basin could not be put under a temporary administrative regime which did not involve a transfer of political sovereignty and which contemplated a final determination of its political connections by popular vote to be taken at a distant date; no free city like Dantzig could be created which was, under elaborate international guarantees, to accept exceptional obligations with regard to the use of its port and exceptional relations with a State of which it was not to form a part; properly safeguarded plebescites could not be provided for where populations were at some future date to make choice what sovereignty they would live under; no certain and uniform method of arbitration could be secured for the settlement of anticipated difficulties of final decision with regard to many matters dealt with in the treaty itself; the long-continued supervision of the task of reparation which Germany was to undertake to complete within the next generation might entirely break down; the reconsideration and revision of administrative arrangements and restrictions which the treaty prescribed but which it was recognized might not prove of lasting advantage or entirely fair if too long enforced would be impracticable. The promises governments were making to one another about the way in which labour was to be dealt with, by law not only but in fact as well, would remain a mere humane thesis if there was to be no common tribunal of opinion and judgment to which liberal statesmen could resort for the influences which alone might secure their redemption. A league of free nations had become a practical necessity. Examine the treaty of peace and you will find that everywhere throughout its manifold provisions its framers have felt obliged to turn to the League of Nations as an indispensable instrumentality for the maintenance of the new order it has been their purpose to set up in the world,—the world of civilized men.

That there should be a league of nations to steady the counsels and maintain the peaceful understandings of the world, to make, not treaties alone, but the accepted principles of international law as well, the actual rule of conduct among the governments of the world, had been one of the agreements accepted from the first as the basis of peace with the central powers. The statesmen of all the belligerent countries were agreed that such a league must be created to sustain the settlements that were to be effected. But at first I think there was a feeling among some of them that, while it must be attempted, the formation of such a league was perhaps a counsel of perfection which practical men, long experienced in the world of affairs, must agree to very cautiously and with many misgivings. It was only as the difficult work of arranging an all but universal adjustment of the world's affairs advanced from day to day from one stage of conference to another that it became evident to them that what they were seeking would be little more than something written upon paper, to be interpreted and applied by such methods as the chances of politics might make available if they did not provide a means of common counsel which all were obliged to accept, a common authority whose decisions would be recognized as decisions which all must respect.

And so the most practical, the most skeptical among them turned more and more to the League as the authority through which international action was to be secured, the authority without which, as they had come to see it, it would be difficult to give assured effect either to this treaty or to any other international understanding upon which they were to depend for the maintenance of peace. The fact that the Covenant of the League was the first substantive part of the treaty to be worked out and agreed upon, while all else was in solution, helped to make the formulation of the rest easier. The Conference was, after all, not to be ephemeral. The concert of nations was to continue, under a definite Covenant which had been agreed upon and which all were convinced was workable. They could go forward with confidence to make arrangements intended to be permanent. The most practical of the conferees were at last the most ready to refer to the League of Nations the superintendence of all interests which did not admit of immediate determination, of all administrative problems which were to require a continuing oversight. What had seemed a counsel of perfection had come to seem a plain counsel of necessity. The League of Nations was the practical statesman's hope of success in many of the most difficult things he was attempting.

And it had validated itself in the thought of every member of the Conference as something much bigger, much greater every way, than a mere instrument for carrying out the provisions of a particular treaty. It was universally recognized that all the peoples of the world demanded of the Conference that it should create such a continuing concert of free nations as would make wars of aggression and spoliation such as this that has just ended forever impossible. A cry had gone out from every home in every stricken land from which sons and brothers and fathers had gone forth to the great sacrifice that such a sacrifice should never again be exacted. It was manifest why it had been exacted. It had been exacted because one nation desired dominion and other nations had known no means of defence except armaments and alliances. War had lain at the heart of every arrangement of the Europe,—of every arrangement of the world,—that preceded the war. Restive peoples had been told that fleets and armies, which they toiled to sustain, meant peace; and they now knew that they they had been lied to: that fleets and armies had been maintained to promote national ambitions and meant war. They knew that no old policy meant anything else but force, force,—always force. And they knew that it was intolerable. Every true heart in the world, and every enlightened judgment demanded that, at whatever cost of independent action, every government that took thought for its people or for justice or for ordered freedom should lend itself to a new purpose and utterly destroy the old order of international politics. Statesmen might see difficulties, but the people could see none and could brook no denial. A war in which they had been bled white to beat the terror that lay concealed in every Balance of Power must not end in a mere victory of arms and a new balance. The monster that had resorted to arms must be put in chains that could not be broken. The united power of free nations must put a stop to aggression, and the world must be given peace. If there was not the will or the intelligence to accomplish that now, there must be another and a final war and the world must be swept clean of every power that could renew the terror. The League of Nations was not merely an instrument to adjust and remedy old wrongs under a new treaty of peace; it was the only hope for mankind. Again and again had the demon of war been cast out of the house of the peoples and the house swept clean by a treaty of peace; only to prepare a time when he would enter in again with spirits worse than himself. The house must now be given a tenant who could hold it against all such. Convenient, indeed indispensable, as statesmen found the newly planned League of Nations to be for the execution of present plans of peace and reparation, they saw it in a new aspect before their work was finished. They saw it as the main object of the peace, as the only thing that could complete it or make it worth while. They saw it as the hope of the world, and that hope they did not dare to disappoint. Shall we or any other free people hesitate to accept this great duty? Dare we reject it and break the heart of the world?

And so the result of the Conference of Peace, so far as Germany is concerned, stands complete. The difficulties encountered were very many. Sometimes they seemed insuperable. It was impossible to accommodate the interests of so great a body of nations,—interests which directly or indirectly affected almost every nation in the world.—without many minor compromises. The treaty, as a result, is not exactly what we would have written. It is probably not what any one of the national delegations would have written. But results were worked out which on the whole bear test. I think that it will be found that the compromises which were accepted as inevitable nowhere cut to the heart of any principle. The work of the Conference squares, as a whole, with the principles agreed upon as the basis of the peace as well as with the practical possibilities of the international situations which had to be faced and dealt with as facts.

I shall presently have occasion to lay before you a special treaty with France, whose object is the temporary protection of France from unprovoked aggression by the Power with whom this treaty of peace has been negotiated. Its terms link it with this treaty. I take the liberty, however, of reserving it for special explication on another occasion.

The rôle which America was to play in the Conference seemed determined, as I have said, before my colleagues and I got to Paris,—determined by the universal expectations of the nations whose representatives, drawn from all quarters of the globe, we were to deal with. It was universally recognized that America had entered the war to promote no private or peculiar interest of her own but only as the champion of rights which she was glad to share with free men and lovers of justice everywhere. We had formulated the principles upon which the settlement was to be made,—the principles upon which the armistice had been agreed to and the parleys of peace undertaken,—and no one doubted that our desire was to see the treaty of peace formulated along the actual lines of those principles,—and desired nothing else. We were welcomed as disinterested friends. We were resorted to as arbiters in many a difficult matter. It was recognized that our material aid would be indispensable in the days to come, when industry and credit would have to be brought back to their normal operation again and communities beaten to the ground assisted to their feet once more, and it was taken for granted, I am proud to say, that we would play the helpful friend in these things as in all others without prejudice or favour. We were generously accepted as the unaffected champions of what was right. It was a very responsible rôle to play; but I am happy to report that the fine group of Americans who helped with their expert advice in each part of the varied settlements sought in every transaction to justify the high confidence reposed in them.

And that confidence, it seems to me, is the measure of our opportunity and of our duty in the days to come, in which the new hope of the peoples of the world is to be fulfilled or disappointed. The fact that America is the friend of the nations, whether they be rivals or associates, is no new fact: it is only the discovery of it by the rest of the world that is new.

America may be said to have just reached her majority as a world power. It was almost exactly twenty-one years ago that the results of the war with Spain put us unexpectedly in possession of rich islands on the other side of the world and brought us into association with other governments in the control of the West Indies. It was regarded as a sinister and ominous thing by the statesmen of more than one European chancellery that we should have extended our power beyond the confines of our continental dominions. They were accustomed to think of new neighbours as a new menace, of rivals as watchful enemies. There were persons amongst us at home who looked with deep disapproval and avowed anxiety on such extensions of our national authority over distant islands and over peoples whom they feared we might exploit, not serve and assist. But we have not exploited them. We have been their friends and have sought to serve them. And our dominion has been a menace to no other nation. We redeemed our honour to the utmost in our dealings with Cuba. She is weak but absolutely free; and it is her trust in us that makes her free. Weak peoples everywhere stand ready to give us any authority among them that will assure them a like friendly oversight and direction. They know that there is no ground for fear in receiving us as their mentors and guides. Our isolation was ended twenty years ago; and now fear of us is ended also, our counsel and association sought after and desired. There can be no question of our ceasing to be a world power. The only question is whether we can refuse the moral leadership that is offered us, whether we shall accept or reject the confidence of the world.

The war and the Conference of Peace now sitting in Paris seem to me to have answered that question. Our participation in the war established our position among the nations and nothing but our own mistaken action can alter it. It was not an accident or a matter of sudden choice that we are no longer isolated and devoted to a policy which has only our own interest and advantage for its object. It was our duty to go in, if we were indeed the champions of liberty and of right. We answered to the call of duty in a way so spirited, so utterly without thought of what we spent of blood or treasure, so effective, so worthy of the admiration of true men everywhere, so wrought out of the stuff of all that was heroic, that the whole world saw at last, in the flesh, in noble action, a great ideal asserted and vindicated, by a nation they had deemed material and now found to be compact of the spiritual forces that must free men of every nation from every unworthy bondage. It is thus that a new role and a new responsibility have come to this great nation that we honour and which we would all wish to lift to yet higher levels of service and achievement.

The stage is set, the destiny disclosed. It has come about by no plan of our conceiving, but by the hand of God who led us into this way. We cannot turn back. We can only go forward, with lifted eyes and freshened spirit, to follow the vision. It was of this that we dreamed at our birth. America shall in truth show the way. The light streams upon the path ahead, and nowhere else.

Herbert Hoover

Principles and Ideals of the United States Government, 1928

M R. HOOVER never used a ghost writer. His principal campaign addresses, therefore, required hard work and usually two or three weeks to prepare. "He would search his storehouse of words," wrote his secretary, Theodore Joslin, "for those that would interpret his exact thought, testing each and every one for stress and strain, and then interlocking them with a fine network of minor words like the web of wires on a suspension bridge." Toward the close of the campaign of 1928 Mr. Hoover determined that the Republican party should draw the issue of the American system, as opposed to all forms of collectivism. "Our managers," he wrote, "thought that the subject was not of much importance or public interest and that harping on it carried liabilities. However, I felt that this infection was around, and I dealt with it definitely." This address was delivered in New York City on October 22 as the principal closing address of the presidential campaign. Though the speech is popularly known as "The Philosophy of Rugged Individualism" from a phrase used in it, the correct title is given above.

I am indebted to The Hoover Institute and Library of Stanford University for lending a page-proof of the first pamphlet issue of the "Address of Mr. Herbert Hoover, Republican Nominee for President, to be delivered at New York, N. Y., Monday evening, October 22, 1928."

ADDRESS

OF

MR. HERBERT HOOVER

Republican Nominee for President

❧❦❧

To be delivered at New York, N. Y.,
Monday evening, October 22, 1928

This campaign now draws near a close. The platforms of the two parties defining principles and offering solutions of various national problems have been presented and are being earnestly considered by our people.

After four months' debate it is not the Republican Party which finds reason for abandonment of any of the principles it has laid down, or of the views it has expressed for solution of the problems before the country. The principles to which it adheres are rooted deeply in the foundations of our national life. The solutions which it proposes are based on experience with government and on a consciousness that it may have the responsibility for placing those solutions in action.

In my acceptance speech I endeavored to outline the spirit and ideals by which I would be guided in carrying that platform into administration. Tonight, I will not deal with the multitude of issues which have been already well canvassed. I intend rather to discuss some of those more fundamental principles and ideals upon which I believe the Government of the United States should be conducted.

The Republican party has ever been a party of progress. I do not need to review its seventy years of constructive history. It has always reflected the spirit of the American people. Never has it done more for the advancement of fundamental progress than during the past seven and a half years since we took over the Government amidst the ruin left by war.

It detracts nothing from the character and energy of the American people, it minimizes in no degree the quality of their accomplishments to say that the policies of the Republican Party have played a large part in recuperation from the war and the building of the magnificent progress which shows upon every hand today. I say with emphasis that without the wise policies which the Republican Party has brought into action during this period, no such progress would have been possible.

The first responsibility of the Republican Administration was to renew the march of progress from its collapse by the war. That task involved the restoration of confidence in the future and the liberation and stimulation of the constructive energies of our people. It discharged that task. There is not a person within the sound of my voice that does not know the profound progress which our country has made in this period. Every man and woman knows that American comfort, hope and confidence for the future are immeasurably higher this day than they were seven and one-half years ago.

It is not my purpose to enter upon a detailed recital of the great constructive measures of the past seven and a half years by which this has been brought about. It is sufficient to remind you of the restoration of employment to the millions who walked your streets in idleness; to remind you of the creation of the budget system; the reduction of six billions of national debt which gave the powerful impulse of that vast sum returned to industry and commerce; the four sequent reductions of taxes and thereby the lift to the living of every family; the enactment of adequate protective tariff and immigration laws which have safeguarded our workers and farmers from floods of goods and labor from foreign countries; the creation of credit facilities and many other aids to agriculture; the building up of foreign trade; the care of veterans; the development of aviation, of radio, of our inland waterways, of our highways; the expansion of scientific research, of welfare activities, the making of safer highways, safer mines, better homes; the spread of outdoor recreation; the improvement in public health and the care of children; and a score of other progressive actions.

Nor do I need to remind you that Government today deals with an economic and social system vastly more intricate and delicately adjusted than ever before. That system now must be kept in perfect tune if we would maintain uninterrupted employment and the high standards of living of our people. The Government has come to touch this delicate web at a thousand points. Yearly the relations of Government to national prosperity become more and more intimate. Only through keen vision and helpful cooperation by the Government has stability in business and stability in employment been maintained during this past seven and a half years. There always are some localities, some industries and some individuals who do not share the prevailing prosperity. The task of government is to lessen these inequalities.

Never has there been a period when the Federal Government has given such aid and impulse to the progress of our people, not alone to economic progress but to the development of those agencies which make for moral and spiritual progress.

But in addition to this great record of contributions of the Republican Party to progress, there has been a further fundamental contribution—a contribution underlying and sustaining all the others—and that is the resistance of the Republican Party to every attempt to inject the Government into business in competition with its citizens.

After the war, when the Republican Party assumed administration of the country, we were faced with the problem of determination of the very nature of our national life. During 150 years we have builded up a form of self-government and a social system which is peculiarly our own. It differs essentially from all others in the world. It is the American system. It is just as definite and positive a political and social system as has ever been developed on earth. It is founded upon a particular conception of self-government; in which decentralized local responsibility is the very base. Further than this, it is founded upon the conception that only through ordered liberty, freedom and equal opportunity to the individual will his initiative and enterprise spur on the march of progress. And in our insistence upon equality of opportunity has our system advanced beyond all the world.

During the war we necessarily turned to the Government to solve every difficult economic problem. The Government having absorbed every energy of our people for war, there was no other solution. For the preservation of the State the Federal Government became a centralized despotism which undertook unprecedented responsibilities, assumed autocratic powers, and took over the business of citizens. To a large degree we regimented our whole people temporarily into a socialistic state. However justified in time of war, if continued in peace time it would destroy not only our American system but with it our progress and freedom as well.

When the war closed, the most vital of all issues both in our own country and throughout the world was whether Governments should continue their wartime ownership and operation of many instrumentalities of production and distribution. We were challenged with a peace-time choice between the American system of rugged individualism and a European philosophy of diametrically opposed doctrines—doctrines of paternalism and state socialism. The acceptance of these ideas would have meant the destruction of self-government through centralization of government. It would have meant the undermining of the individual initiative and enterprise through which our people have grown to unparalleled greatness.

The Republican Party from the beginning resolutely turned its face away from these ideas and these war practices. A Republican Congress cooperated with the Democratic administration to demobilize many of our war activities. At that time the two parties were accord upon that point. When the Republican Party came into full power it went at once resolutely back to our fundamental conception of the state and the rights and responsibilities of the individual. Thereby it restored confidence and hope in the American people, it freed and stimulated enterprise, it restored the Government to its position as an umpire instead of a player in the economic game. For these reasons the American people have gone forward in progress while the rest of the world has halted, and some countries have even gone backwards. If anyone will study the causes of retarded recuperation in Europe, he will find much of it due to the stifling of private initiative on one hand, and overloading of the Government with business on the other.

There has been revived in this campaign, however, a series of proposals which, if adopted, would be a long step toward the abandonment of our American system and a surrender to the destructive operation of governmental conduct of commercial business. Because the country is faced with difficulty and doubt over certain national problems—that is, prohibition, farm relief and electrical power—our opponents propose that we must thrust government a long way into the businesses which give rise to these problems. In effect, they abandon the tenets of their own party and turn to state socialism as a solution for the difficulties presented by all three. It is proposed that we shall change from prohibition to the state purchase and sale of liquor. If their agricultural relief program means anything, it means that the Government shall directly or indirectly buy and sell and fix prices of agricultural products. And we are to go into the hydroelectric-power business. In other words, we are confronted with a huge program of government in business.

There is, therefore, submitted to the American people a question of fundamental principle. That is: shall we depart from the principles of our American political and economic system, upon which we have advanced beyond all the rest of the world, in order to adopt methods based on principles destructive of its very foundations? And I wish to emphasize the seriousness of these proposals. I wish to make my position clear; for this goes to the very roots of American life and progress.

I should like to state to you the effect that this projection of government in business would have upon our system of self-government and our economic system. That effect would reach to the daily life of every man and woman. It would impair the very basis of liberty and freedom not only for those left outside the fold of expanded bureaucracy but for those embraced within it.

Let us first see the effect upon self-government. When the Federal Government undertakes to go into commercial business it must at once set up the organization and administration of that business, and it immediately finds itself in a labyrinth, every alley of which leads to the destruction of self-governmnt.

Commercial business requires a concentration of responsibility. Self-government requires decentralization and many checks and balances to safeguard liberty. Our Government to succeed in business would need become in effect a despotism. There at once begins the destruction of self-government.

The first problem of the government about to adventure in commercial business is to determine a method of administration. It must secure leadership and direction. Shall this leadership be chosen by political agencies or shall we make it elective? The hard practical fact is that leadership in business must come through the sheer rise in ability and character. That rise can only take place in the free atmosphere of competition. Competition is closed by bureaucracy. Political agencies are feeble channels through which to select able leaders to conduct commercial business.

Government, in order to avoid the possible incompetence, corruption and tyranny of too great authority in individuals entrusted with commercial business, inevitably turns to boards and commissions. To make sure that there are checks and balances, each member of such boards and commissions must have equal authority. Each has his separate responsibility to the public, and at once we have the conflict of ideas and the lack of decision which would ruin any commercial business. It has contributed greatly to the demoralization of our shipping business. Moreover, these commissions must be representative of different sections and different political parties, so that at once we have an entire blight upon coordinated action within their ranks which destroys any possibility of effective administration.

Moreover, our legislative bodies cannot in fact delegate their full authority to commissions or to individuals for the conduct of matters vital to the American people; for if we would preserve government by the people we must preserve the authority of our legislators in the activities of our government.

Thus every time the Federal Government goes into a commercial business, 531 Senators and Congressmen become the actual board of directors of that business. Every time a state government goes into business one or two hundred state senators and legislators become the actual directors of that business. Even if they were supermen and if there were no politics in the United States, no body of such numbers could competently direct commercial activities; for that requires initiative, instant decision, and action. It took Congress six years of constant discussion to even decide what the method of administration of Muscle Shoals should be.

When the Federal Government undertakes to go into business, the state governments are at once deprived of control and taxation of that business; when a state government undertakes to go into business, it at once deprives the municipalities of taxation and control of that business. Municipalities, being local and close to the people, can, at times, succeed in business where Federal and State Governments must fail.

We have trouble enough with log rolling in legislative bodies today. It originates naturally from desires of citizens to advance their particular section or to secure some necessary service. It would be multiplied a thousandfold were the Federal and state governments in these businesses.

The effect upon our economic progress would be even worse. Business progressiveness is dependent on competition. New methods and new ideas are the outgrowth of the spirit of adventure, of individual initiative and of individual enterprise. Without adventure there is no progress. No government administration can rightly take chances with taxpayers' money.

There is no better example of the practical incompetence of government to conduct business than the history of our railways. During the war the government found it necessary to operate the railways. That operation continued until after the war. In the year before being freed from Government operation they were not able to meet the demands for transportation. Eight years later we find them under private enterprise transporting 15 per cent more goods and meeting every demand for service. Rates have been reduced by 15 per cent and net earnings increased from less than 1 per cent on their valuation to about 5 per cent. Wages of employees have improved by 13 per cent. The wages of railway employees are today 121 per cent above pre-war, while the wages of Government employees are today only 65 per cent above pre-war. That should be a sufficient commentary upon the efficiency of Government operation.

Let us now examine this question from the point of view of the person who may get a Government job and is admitted into the the new bureaucracy. Upon that subject let me quote from a speech of that great leader of labor, Samuel Gompers, delivered in Montreal in 1920, a few years before his death. He said:

"I believe there is no man to whom I would take second position in my loyalty to the Republic of the United States, and yet I would not give it more power over the individual citizenship of our country. * * *

"It is a question of whether it shall be Government ownership or private ownership under control. * * * If I were in the minority of one in this convention, I would want to cast my vote so that the men of labor shall not willingly enslave themselves to Government authority in their industrial effort for freedom. * * *

"Let the future tell the story of who is right or who is wrong; who has stood for freedom and who has been willing to submit their fate industrially to the Government."

I would amplify Mr. Gompers' statement. The great body of Government employees which would be created by the proposals of our opponents would either comprise a political machine at the disposal of the party in power, or alternatively, to prevent this, the Government by stringent civil-service rules must debar its employes from their full political rights as free men. It must limit them in the liberty to bargain for their own wages, for no Government employee can strike against his Government and thus against the whole people. It makes a legislative body with all its political currents their final employer and master. Their bargaining does not rest upon economic need or economic strength but on political potence.

But what of those who are outside the bureaucracy? What is the effect upon their lives?

The area of enterprise and opportunity for them to strive and rise is at once limited.

The Government in commercial business does not tolerate amongst its customers the freedom of competitive reprisals to which private business is subject. Bureaucracy does not tolerate the spirit of independence; it spreads the spirit of submission into our daily life and penetrates the temper of our people not with the habit of powerful resistance to wrong but with the habit of timid acceptance of irresistible might.

Bureaucracy is ever desirous of spreading its influence and its power. You cannot extend the mastery of the government over the daily working life of a people without at the same time making it the master of the people's souls and thoughts. Every expansion of government in business means that government in order to protect itself from the political consequences of its errors and wrongs is driven irresistibly without peace to greater and greater control of the nations' press and platform. Free speech does not live many hours after free industry and free commerce die.

It is a false liberalism that interprets itself into the Government operation of commercial business. Every step of bureaucratizing of the business of our country poisons the very roots of liberalism—that is, political equality, free speech, free assembly, free press, and equality of opportunity. It is the road not to more liberty, but to less liberty. Liberalism should be found not striving to spread bureaucracy but striving to set bounds to it. True liberalism seeks all legitimate freedom first in the confident belief that without such freedom the pursuit of all other blessings and benefits is vain. That belief is the foundation of all American progress, political as well as economic.

Liberalism is a force truly of the spirit, a force proceeding from the deep realization that economic freedom cannot be sacrificed if political freedom is to be preserved. Even if governmental conduct of business could give us more efficiency instead of less efficiency, the fundamental objection to it would remain unaltered and unabated. It would destroy political equality. It would increase rather than decrease abuse and corruption. It would stifle initiative and invention. It would undermine the development of leadership. It would cramp and cripple the mental and spiritual energies of our people. It would extinguish equality and opportunity. It would dry up the spirit of liberty and progress. For these reasons primarily it must be resisted. For a hundred and fifty years liberalism has found its true spirit in the American system, not in the European systems.

I do not wish to be misunderstood in this statement. I am defining a general policy. It does not mean that our government is to part with one iota of its national resources without complete protection to the public interest. I have already stated that where the government is engaged in public works for purposes of flood control, of navigation, of irrigation, of scientific research or national defense, or in pioneering a new art, it will at times necessarily produce power or commodities as a by-product. But they must be a by-product of the major purpose, not the major purpose itself.

Nor do I wish to be misinterpreted as believing that the United States is free-for-all and devil-take-the-hindmost. The very essence of equality of opportunity and of American individualism is that there shall be no domination by any group or combination in this Republic, whether it be business or political. On the contrary, it demands economic justice as well as political and social justice. It is no system of laissez faire.

I feel deeply on this subject because during the war I had some practical experience with governmental operation and control. I have witnessed not only at home but abroad the many failures of government in business.

I have seen its tyrannies, its injustices, its destructions of self-government, its undermining of the very instincts which carry our people forward to progress. I have witnessed the lack of advance, the lowered standards of living, the depressed spirits of people working under such a system. My objection is based not upon theory or upon a failure to recognize wrong or abuse, but I know the adoption of such methods would strike at the very roots of American life and would destroy the very basis of American progress.

Our people have the right to know whether we can continue to solve our great problems without abandonment of our American system. I know we can. We have demonstrated that our system is responsive enough to meet any new and intricate development in our economic and business life. We have demonstrated that we can meet any economic problem and still maintain our democracy as master in its own house and that we can at the same time preserve equality of opportunity and individual freedom.

In the last fifty years we have discovered that mass production will produce articles for us at half the cost they required previously. We have seen the resultant growth of large units of production and distribution. This is big business. Many businesses must be bigger for our tools are bigger, our country is bigger. We now build a single dynamo of a hundred thousand horsepower. Even fifteen years ago that would have been a big business all by itself. Yet today advance in production requires that we set ten of these units together in a row.

The American people from bitter experience have a rightful fear that great business units might be used to dominate our industrial life and by illegal and unethical practices destroy equality of opportunity.

Years ago the Republican Administration established the principle that such evils could be corrected by regulation. It developed methods by which abuses could be prevented while the full value of industrial progress could be retained for the public. It insisted upon the principle that when great public utilities were clothed with the security of partial monopoly, whether it be railways, power plants, telephones or what not, then there must be the fullest and most complete control of rates, services, and finances by government or local agencies.

It declared that these businesses must be conducted with glass pockets.

As to our great manufacturing and distributing industries, the Republican Party insisted upon the enactment of laws that not only would maintain competition but would destroy conspiracies to destroy the smaller units or dominate and limit the equality of opportunity amongst our people.

One of the great problems of government is to determine to what extent the Government shall regulate and control commerce and industry and how much it shall leave it alone. No system is perfect. We have had many abuses in the private conduct of business. That every good citizen resents. It is just as important that business keep out of government as that government keep out of business.

Nor am I setting up the contention that our institutions are perfect. No human ideal is ever perfectly attained, since humanity itself is not perfect.

The wisdom of our forefathers in their conception that progress can only be attained as the sum of the accomplishment of free individuals has been re-enforced by all of the great leaders of the country since that day. Jackson, Lincoln, Cleveland, McKinley, Roosevelt, Wilson, and Coolidge have stood unalterably for these principles.

And what have been the results of our American system? Our country has become the land of opportunity to those born without inheritance, not merely because of the wealth of its resources and industry but because of this freedom of initiative and enterprise. Russia has natural resources equal to ours. Her people are equally industrious, but she has not had the blessings of 150 years of our form of government and of our social system.

By adherence to the principles of decentralized self-government, ordered liberty, equal opportunity and freedom to the individual our American experiment in human welfare has yielded a degree of well-being unparalleled in all the world. It has come nearer to the abolition of poverty, to the abolition of fear of want, than humanity has ever reached before. Progress of the past seven years is the proof of it. This alone furnishes the answer to our opponents who ask us to introduce destructive elements into the system by which this has been accomplished.

Let us see what this system has done for us in our recent years of difficult and trying reconstruction and let us then solemnly ask ourselves if we now wish to abandon it.

As a nation we came out of the war with great losses. We made no profits from it. The apparent increases in wages were at that time fictitious. We were poorer as a nation when we emerged from the war. Yet during these last eight years we have recovered from these losses and increased our national income by over one-third even if we discount the inflation of the dollar. That there has been a wide diffusion of our gain in wealth and income is marked by a hundred proofs. I know of no better test of the improved conditions of the average family than the combined increase in assets of life and industrial insurance, building and loan associations, and savings deposits. These are the savings banks of the average man. These agencies alone have in seven years increased by nearly 100 per cent to the gigantic sum of over 50 billions of dollars, or nearly one-sixth of our whole national wealth. We have increased in home ownership, we have expanded the investments of the average man.

In addition to these evidences of larger savings, our people are steadily increasing their spending for higher standards of living. Today there are almost 9 automobiles for each 10 families, where seven and a half years ago only enough automobiles were running to average less than 4 for each 10 families. The slogan of progress is changing from the full dinner pail to the full garage. Our people have more to eat, better things to wear, and better homes. We have even gained in elbow room, for the increase of residential floor space is over 25 per cent with less than 10 per cent increase in our number of people. Wages have increased, the cost of living has decreased. The job to every man and woman has been made more secure. We have in this short period decreased the fear of poverty, the fear of unemployment, the fear of old age; and these are fears that are the greatest calamities of human kind.

All this progress means far more than greater creature comforts. It finds a thousand interpretations into a greater and fuller life. A score of new helps save the drudgery of the home. In seven years we have added 70 per cent to the electric power at the elbow of our workers and further promoted them from carriers of burdens to directors of machines. We have steadily reduced the sweat in human labor. Our hours of labor are lessened; our leisure has increased. We have expanded our parks and playgrounds. We have nearly doubled our attendance at games. We pour into outdoor recreation in every direction. The visitors at our national parks have trebled and we have so increased the number of sportsmen fishing in our streams and lakes that the longer time between bites is becoming a political issue. In these seven and one-half years the radio has brought music and laughter, education and political discussion to almost every fireside.

Springing from our prosperity with its greater freedom, its vast endowment of scientific research and the greater resources with which to care for public health, we have according to our insurance actuaries during this short period since the war lengthened the average span of life by nearly eight years. We have reduced infant mortality, we have vastly decreased the days of illness and suffering in the life of every man and woman. We have improved the facilities for the care of the crippled and helpless and deranged.

From our increasing resources we have expanded our educational system in eight years from an outlay of 1,200 millions to 2,700 millions of dollars. The education of our youth has become almost our largest and certainly our most important activity. From our greater income and thus our ability to free youth from toil we have increased the attendance in our grade schools by 14 per cent, in our high schools by 80 per cent, and in our institutions of higher learning by 95 per cent. Today we have more youth in these institutions of higher learning twice over than all the rest of the world put together. We have made notable progress in literature, in art and in public taste.

We have made progress in the leadership of every branch of American life. Never in our history was the leadership in our economic life more distinguished in its abilities than today, and it has grown greatly in its consciousness of public responsibility. Leadership in our professions—and in moral and spiritual affairs of our country was never of a higher order. And our magnificent educational system is bringing forward a host of recruits for the succession to this leadership.

I do not need to recite more figures and more evidence. I cannot believe that the American people wish to abandon or in any way to weaken the principles of economic freedom and self-government which have been maintained by the Republican Party and which have produced results so amazing and so stimulating to the spiritual as well as to the material advance of the nation.

Your city has been an outstanding beneficiary of this great progress and of these safeguarded principles. With its suburbs it has, during the last seven and a half years, grown by over a million and a half of people until it has become the largest metropolitan district of all the world. Here you have made abundant opportunity not only for the youth of the land but for the immigrant from foreign shores. This city is the commercial center of the United States. It is the commercial agent of the American people. It is a great organism of specialized skill and leadership in finance, industry and commerce, which reaches every spot in our country. Its progress and its beauty are the pride of the whole American people. It leads our nation in its benevolences to charity, to education and scientific research. It is the center of art, music, literature and drama. It has come to have a more potent voice than any other city in the United States.

But when all is said and done the very life, progress and prosperity of this city is wholly dependent on the prosperity of the 115,000,000 people who dwell in our mountains and valleys across the 3,000 miles to the Pacific Ocean. Every activity of this city is sensitive to every evil and every favorable tide that sweeps this great nation of ours. Be there a slackening of industry in any place it affects New York far more than any other part of the country. In a time of depression one-quarter of all the unemployed in the United States can be numbered in this city. In a time of prosperity the citizens of the great interior of our country pour into your city for business and entertainment at the rate of 150,000 a day. In fact, so much is this city the reflex of the varied interests of our country that the concern of every one of your citizens for national stability, for national prosperity, for national progress, for preservation of our

American system, is far greater than that of any other single part of our country.

We still have great problems if we would achive the full economic advancement of our country. In these past few years some groups in our country have lagged behind others in the march of progress. I refer more particularly to those engaged in the textile, coal and in the agricultural industries. We can assist in solving these problems by cooperation of our Government. To the agricultural industry we shall need to advance initial capital to assist them to stabilize their industry. But this proposal implies that they shall conduct it themselves, and not by the Government. It is in the interest of our cities that we shall bring agriculture and all industries into full stability and prosperity. I know you will gladly cooperate in the faith that in the common prosperity of our country lies its future.

In bringing this address to a conclusion I should like to restate to you some of the fundamental things I have endeavored to bring out.

The foundations of progress and prosperity are dependent as never before upon the wise policies of government, for government now touches at a thousand points the intricate web of economic and social life.

Under administration by the Republican Party in the last 7½ years our country as a whole has made unparalleled progress and this has been in generous part reflected to this great city. Prosperity is no idle expression. It is a job for every worker; it is the safety and the safeguard of every business and every home. A continuation of the policies of the Republican Party is fundamentally necessary to the further advancement of this progress and to the further building up of this prosperity.

I have dwelt at some length on the principles of relationship between the Government and business. I make no apologies for dealing with this subject. The first necessity of any nation is the smooth functioning of the vast business machinery for employment, feeding, clothing, housing and providing luxuries and comforts to a people. Unless these basic elements are properly organized and function, there can be no progress in business, in education, literature, music or art. There can be no advance in the fundamental ideals of a people. A people cannot make progress in poverty.

I have endeavored to present to you that the greatness of America has grown out of a political and social system and a method of control of economic forces distinctly its own—our American system—which has carried this great experiment in human welfare farther than ever before in all history. We are nearer today to the ideal of the abolition of poverty and fear from the lives of men and women than ever before in any land. And I again repeat that the departure from our American system by injecting principles destructive to it which our opponents propose will jeopardize the very liberty and freedom of our people, will destroy equality of opportunity not alone to ourselves but to our children.

To me the foundation of American life rests upon the home and the family. I read into these great economic forces, these intricate and delicate relations of the Government with business and with our political and social life, but one supreme end—that we reinforce the ties that bind together the millions of our families, that we strengthen the security, the happiness and the independence of every home.

My conception of America is a land where men and women may walk in ordered freedom in the independent conduct of their occupations; where they may enjoy the advantages of wealth, not concentrated in the hands of the few but spread through the lives of all, where they build and safeguard their homes, and give to their children the fullest advantages and opportunities of American life; where every man shall be respected in the faith that his conscience and his heart direct him to follow; where a contented and happy people, secure in their liberties, free from poverty and fear, shall have the leisure and impulse to seek a fuller life.

Some may ask where all this may lead beyond mere material progress. It leads to a release of the energies of men and women from the dull drudgery of life to a wider vision and a higher hope. It leads to the opportunity for greater and greater service, not alone from man to man in our own land, but from our country to the whole world. It leads to an America, healthy in body, healthy in spirit, unfettered, youthful, eager—with a vision searching beyond the farthest horizons, with an open mind sympathetic and generous. It is to these higher ideals and for these purposes that I pledge myself and the Republican Party.

Franklin D. Roosevelt

The Philosophy of Government, 1932

I N THE CAMPAIGN of 1932 the Democratic candidate for the
presidency made twelve major speeches, sixty-seven secondary
speeches, and innumerable "appearances." From September 12
to November 7 he traveled thirteen thousand miles. The Commonwealth Club speech, "The Philosophy of Government," is regarded
as one of the best he ever delivered. Originally Mr. Roosevelt had
planned to visit this prominent San Francisco club at noon on September 23 and to speak briefly. His advisers, aware that the membership of the Club embraced a group of extraordinarily intelligent
men who were interested in discussing national issues on a nonpar-
tisan basis, urged Mr. Roosevelt to undertake a major address. For
some months the candidate had had in mind the delivering of a full-
dress speech upon his political philosophy, and this occasion seemed
to furnish an ideal opportunity. Roosevelt worked hard upon the
address, making final changes as late as two in the morning of the
day of its presentation.

This is a facsimile of the first printing of this address, issued by
the Democratic National Committee, New York City. A copy of
this first edition was presented to the Huntington Library by the
Franklin D. Roosevelt Library, Hyde Park. In *The Public Papers
and Addresses of Franklin D. Roosevelt*, Vol. I, this speech is
labelled "Campaign Address on Progressive Government."

The
PHILOSOPHY
OF
GOVERNMENT

Governor
Franklin D. Roosevelt's
Speech

at

The Commonwealth Club
San Francisco, California
September 23, 1932

★

Issued by
THE DEMOCRATIC NATIONAL COMMITTEE
Hotel Biltmore, New York City

I COUNT it a privilege to be invited to address the Commonwealth Club. It has stood in the life of this city and State, and, it is perhaps accurate to add, the nation, as a group of citizen leaders interested in fundamental problems of government and chiefly concerned with achievement of progress in government through non-partisan means.

The privilege of addressing you, therefore, in the heat of a political campaign, is great. I want to respond to your courtesy in terms consistent with your policy.

I WANT to speak not of politics but of government. I want to speak not of parties but of universal principles. They are not political except in that large sense in which a great American once expressed a definition of politics—that nothing **Not Speaking** in all of human life is foreign to the **of Politics** science of politics.

I do want to give you, however, a recollection of a long life spent, for a large part, in public office. Some of my conclusions and observations have been deeply accentuated in these past few weeks.

I have traveled far—from Albany to the Golden Gate. I have seen many people, and heard many things, and today, when, in a sense, my journey has reached the halfway mark, I am glad of the opportunity to discuss with you what it all means to me.

Sometimes, my friends, particularly in years such as these, the hand of discouragement falls upon us. It seems that things are in a rut, fixed, settled, that the world has grown old and tired and very much out of joint. This is the mood of depression, of dire and weary depression.

BUT then we look around us in America, and everything tells us that we are wrong. America is new. It is in the process of change and development. It has the great potentialities of youth, and particularly is

"America Is New" this true of the great West and of this coast and of California.

I would not have you feel that I regard this in any sense a new community. I have traveled in many parts of the world, but never have I felt more the arresting thought of the change and development more than here, where the old, mystic East would seem to be near to us, where the currents of life and thought and commerce of the whole world meet us. This factor alone is sufficient to cause man to stop and think of the deeper meaning of things when he stands in this community.

But, more than that, I appreciate that the membership of this club consists of men who are thinking in terms beyond the immediate present, beyond their own immediate tasks, beyond their own individual interest.

I want to invite you, therefore, to consider with me in the large some of the relationships of government and economic life that go deep into our daily lives, our happiness, our future and our security.

THE issue of government has always been whether individual men and women will have to serve some system of government or economics or whether a system of government and economics exists to serve individual men and women.

Men or System? This question has persistently dominated the discussions of government for many generations. On questions relating to these things men have differed, and for time immemorial it is probable that honest men will continue to differ.

The final word belongs to no man; yet we can still believe in change and in progress. Democracy, as a dear old friend of mine in Indiana, Meredith Nicholson, has called it, is a quest, a never-ending seeking for better things, and in the seeking for these things and the striving for them there are many roads to follow.

But if we map the course of these roads, we find that there are only two general directions.

When we look about us we are likely to forget how hard people have worked to win the privilege of government.

THE growth of the national governments of Europe was a struggle for the development of a centralized force in the nation, strong enough to impose peace upon ruling barons. In many instances the victory of the central government, the creation of a strong central government, was a haven of refuge to the individual. The people preferred the master far away to the exploitation and cruelty of the smaller master near at hand.

Growth of Central Government

But the creators of national government were perforce ruthless men. They were often cruel in their methods, but they did strive steadily toward something that society needed and very much wanted—a strong central State, able to keep the peace, to stamp out civil war, to put the unruly nobleman in his place and to permit the bulk of individuals to live safely.

The man of ruthless force had his place in developing a pioneer country, just as he did in fixing the power of the central government in the development of the nations. Society paid him well for his services and its development. When the development among the nations of Europe, however, had been completed, ambition and ruthlessness, having served its term, tended to overstep its mark.

THERE came a growing feeling that government was conducted for the benefit of a few who thrived unduly at the expense of all. The people sought a balancing—a limiting force. There came gradually, through town councils, trade guilds, national parliaments, by constitutions and by popular participation and control, limitations on arbitrary power.

Government for the Few

Another factor that tended to limit the power of those who ruled was the rise of the ethical conception that a ruler bore a responsibility for the welfare of his subjects.

The American colonies were born in this struggle. The American Revolution was a turning point in it. After the Revolution the struggle continued and shaped itself in the public life of the country.

There were those who, because they had seen the confusion which attended the years of war for American independence, surrendered to the belief that popular government was essentially dangerous and essentially unworkable.

They were honest people, my friends, and we cannot deny that their experience had warranted some measure of fear.

THE most brilliant, honest and able exponent of this point of view was Hamilton. He was too impatient of slow-moving methods.

Fundamentally he believed that the safety of the Republic lay in the autocratic strength of its government, that the **Refers to** destiny of individuals was to serve **Hamilton** that government and that fundamentally a great and strong group of central institutions, guided by a small group of able and public-spirited citizens, could best direct all government.

But Mr. Jefferson, in the Summer of 1776, after drafting the Declaration of Independence, turned his mind to the same problem and took a different view.

He did not deceive himself with outward forms. Government to him was a means to an end, not an end in itself; it might be either a refuge and a help or a threat and a danger, depending on the circumstances.

We find him carefully analyzing the society for which he was to organize a government:

"WE have no paupers—the great mass of our population is of laborers, our rich who cannot live without labor, either manual or professional, being

The Jeffersonian Idea few and of moderate wealth. Most of the laboring class possess property, cultivate their own lands, have families and from the demands for their labor are enabled to exact from the rich and the competent such prices as enable them to feed abundantly, clothe above mere decency, to labor moderately and raise their families."

These people, he considered, had two sets of rights, those of "personal competency" and those involved in acquiring and possessing property.

By "personal competency" he meant the right of free thinking, freedom of forming and expressing opinions and freedom of personal living, each man according to his own lights.

To insure the first set of rights a government must so order its functions as not to interfere with the individual.

But even Jefferson realized that the exercise of the property rights might so interfere with the rights of the individual that the government, without whose assistance the property rights could not exist, must intervene, not to destroy individualism but to protect it.

YOU are familiar with the great political duel which followed; and how Hamilton and his friends, building toward a dominant, centralized power, were at length defeated in the great election of 1800 by Mr. Jefferson's party. Out **Origin of Parties** of that duel came the two parties, Republican and Democratic, as we know them today.

So began, in American political life, the new day, the day of the individual against the system, the day in which individualism was made the great watchword of American life.

The happiest of economic conditions made that day long and splendid. On the western frontier land was substantially free. No one who did not shirk the task of earning a living was entirely without opportunity to do so. Depressions could, and did, come and go; but they could not alter the fundamental fact that most of the people lived partly by selling their labor and partly by extracting their livelihood from the soil, so that starvation and dislocation were practically impossible.

At the very worst there was always the possibility of climbing into a covered wagon and moving West, where the untilled prairies afforded a haven for men to whom the East did not provide a place.

SO great were our natural resources that we could offer this relief not only to our own people but to the distressed of all the world. We could invite immigration from Europe and welcome it with open arms.

The Days of Expansion Traditionally, when a depression came a new section of land was opened in the West. And even our temporary misfortune served our manifest destiny.

IT was in the middle of the nineteenth century that a new force was released and a new dream created. The force was what is called the industrial revolution, the advance of steam and machinery and the rise of the forerunners of the modern industrial plant.

The Industrial Revolution The dream was the dream of an economic machine, able to raise the standard of living for every one; to bring luxury within the reach of the humblest; to annihilate distance by steam power and later by electricity, and to release every one from the drudgery of the heaviest manual toil.

It was to be expected that this would necessarily affect government. Heretofore, government had merely been called upon to produce conditions within which people could live happily, labor peacefully and rest secure. Now it was called upon to aid in the consummation of this new dream.

There was, however, a shadow over the dream. To be made real it required use of the talents of men of tremendous will and tremendous ambition, since by no other force could the problems of financing and engineering and new developments be brought to a consummation.

So manifest were the advantages of the machine age, however, that the United States fearlessly, cheerfully and, I think, rightly accepted the bitter with the sweet.

It was thought that no price was too high to pay for the advantages which we could draw from a finished industrial system.

THE history of the last half century is accordingly in large measure a history of a group of financial titans, whose methods were not scrutinized with too much care and who were honored in proportion as they produced the results, irrespective of the means they used.

Tells of Titans

The financiers who pushed the railroads to the Pacific were always ruthless, often wasteful and frequently corrupt, but they did build railroads and we have them today.

It has been estimated that the American investor paid for the American railway system more than three times over in the process, but despite this fact the net advantage was to the United States.

As long as we had free land, as long as population was growing by leaps and bounds, as long as our industrial plants were insufficient to supply our own needs, society chose to give the ambitious man free play and unlimited reward, provided only that he produced the economic plant so much desired.

DURING this period of expansion there was equal opportunity for all, and the business of government was not to interfere but to assist in the development of industry.

"Fostering Infant Industry"   This was done at the request of business men themselves. The tariff was originally imposed for the purpose of "fostering our infant industry," a phrase I think the older among you will remember as a political issue not so long ago.

The railroads were subsidized, sometimes by grants of money, oftener by grants of land. Some of the most valuable oil lands in the United States were granted to assist the financing of the railroad which pushed through the Southwest.

A nascent merchant marine was assisted by grants of money or by mail subsidies, so that our steam shipping might ply the seven seas.

Some of my friends tell me that they do not want the government in business. With this I agree, but I wonder whether they realize the implications of the past.

For while it has been American doctrine that the government must not go into business in competition with private enterprises, still it has been traditional, particularly in Republican administrations, for business urgently to ask the government to put at private disposal all kinds of government assistance.

THE same man who tells you that he does not want to see the government interfere in business—and he means it and has plenty of good reasons for saying so—is the first to go to Washington and ask the government for a prohibitory tariff on his product.

Looking to Washington   When things get just bad enough —as they did two years ago—he will go with equal speed to the United States Government and ask for a loan. And the Reconstruction Finance

Corporation is the outcome of it.

Each group has sought protection from the government for its own special interests without realizing that the function of government must be to favor no small group at the expense of its duty to protect the rights of personal freedom and of private property of all its citizens.

In retrospect we can now see that the turn of the tide came with the turn of the century. We were reaching our last frontier; there was no more free land and our industrial combinations had become great uncontrolled and irresponsible units of power within the State.

CLEAR-SIGHTED men saw with fear the danger that opportunity would no longer be equal; that the growing corporation, like the feudal baron of old, might threaten the economic freedom of individuals to earn a living. In that hour our anti-trust laws were born.

Threat to Economic Freedom

The cry was raised against the great corporations. Theodore Roosevelt, the first great Republican Progressive, fought a Presidential campaign on the issue of "trust busting" and talked freely about malefactors of great wealth. If the government had a policy it was rather to turn the clock back, to destroy the large combinations and to return to the time when every man owned his individual small business.

This was impossible. Theodore Roosevelt, abandoning the idea of "trust busting," was forced to work out a difference between "good" trusts and "bad" trusts.

The Supreme Court set forth the famous "rule of reason" by which it seems to have meant that a concentration of industrial power was permissible if the method by which it got its power, and the use it made of that power, was reasonable.

WOODROW WILSON, elected in 1912, saw the situation more clearly. Where Jefferson had feared the encroachment of political power on the lives of individuals, Wilson knew that the new power was financial. He saw, in the highly

Wilson Saw Clearly centralized economic system, the despot of the twentieth century, on whom great masses of individuals relied for their safety and their livelihood, and whose irresponsibility and greed (if it were not controlled) would reduce them to starvation and penury.

The concentration of financial power had not proceeded as far in 1912 as it has today, but it had grown far enough for Mr. Wilson to realize fully its implications.

It is interesting, now, to read his speeches. What is called "radical" today (and I have reason to know whereof I speak) is mild compared to the campaign of Mr. Wilson.

"No man can deny," he said, "that the lines of endeavor have more and more narrowed and stiffened; no man who knows anything about the development of industry in this country can have failed to observe the larger kinds of credit are more and more difficult to obtain unless you obtain them upon terms of uniting your efforts with those who already control the industry of the country, and nobody can fail to observe that every man who tries to set himself up in competition with any process of manufacture which has taken place under the control of large combinations of capital will presently find himself either squeezed out or obliged to sell and allow himself to be absorbed."

HAD there been no World War—had Mr. Wilson been able to devote eight years to domestic instead of to international affairs—we might have had a wholly different situation at the present time.

The World War However, the then distant roar of European cannon, growing ever louder, forced him to abandon the study of this issue.

The problem he saw so clearly is left with us as a legacy; and no one of us on either side of the political controversy can deny that it is a matter of grave concern to the government.

A glance at the situation today only too clearly indicates that equality of opportunity as we have known it no longer exists. Our industrial plant is built. The problem just now is whether, under existing conditions, it is not overbuilt.

OUR last frontier has long since been reached, and there is practically no more free land. More than half of our people do not live on the farms or on lands and cannot derive a living by cultivating their own property.

The Last Frontier There is no safety valve in the form of a Western prairie to which those thrown out of work by the Eastern economic machines can go for a new start. We are not able to invite the immigration from Europe to share our endless plenty. We are now providing a drab living for our own people.

Our system of constantly rising tariffs has at last reacted against us to the point of closing our Canadian frontier on the north, our European markets on the east, many of our Latin-American markets to the south and a goodly proportion of our Pacific markets on the west through the retaliatory tariffs of those countries.

It has forced many of our great industrial institutions, who exported their surplus production to such countries, to establish plants in such countries, within the tariff walls.

This has resulted in the reduction of the operation of their American plants and opportunity for employment.

JUST as freedom to farm has ceased, so also the opportunity in business has narrowed. It still is true that men can start small enterprises, trusting to native shrewdness and ability to keep abreast of competitors; but area after area has been pre-empted altogether by the great corporations, and even in the fields which still have no great concerns the small man starts under a handicap.

Narrowing Opportunity The unfeeling statistics of the past three decades show that the independent business man is running a losing race. Perhaps he is forced to the wall; perhaps he cannot command credit; perhaps he is "squeezed out," in Mr. Wilson's words, by highly organized corporate competitors, as your corner grocery man can tell you.

Recently a careful study was made of the concentration of business in the United States.

It showed that our economic life was dominated by some 600-odd corporations who controlled two-thirds of American industry. Ten million small business men divided the other third.

More striking still, it appeared that, if the process of concentration goes on at the same rate, at the end of another century we shall have all American industry controlled by a dozen corporations and run by perhaps a hundred men.

Put plainly, we are steering a steady course toward economic oligarchy, if we are not there already.

CLEARLY, all this calls for a reappraisal of values. A mere builder of more industrial plants, a creator of more railroad systems, an organizer of more corporations, is as likely to be a danger as a help.

Calls for Reappraisal The day of the great promoter or the financial titan, to whom we granted anything if only he would build or develop, is over. Our task now is not discovery or exploitation of natural resources or necessarily producing more goods.

It is the soberer, less dramatic business of administering resources and plants already in hand, of seeking to re-establish foreign markets for our surplus production, of meeting the problem of under-consumption, of adjusting production to consumption, of distributing wealth and products more equitably, of adapting existing economic organizations to the service of the people.

The day of enlightened administration has come.

Just as in older times the central government was first a haven of refuge and then a threat, so now in a closer economic system the central and ambitious financial unit is no longer a servant of national desire but a danger. I would draw the parallel one step further. We did not think because national government had become a threat in the eighteenth century that therefore we should abandon the principle of national government.

Nor today should we abandon the principle of strong economic units called corporations merely because their power is susceptible of easy abuse.

In other times we dealt with the problem of an unduly ambitious central government by modifying it gradually into a constitutional democratic government. So today we are modifying and controlling our economic units.

AS I see it, the task of government in its relation to business is to assist the development of an economic declaration of rights, an economic constitutional order. This is the common task of statesman and business man. It is the minimum requirement of a more permanently safe order of things.

New Declaration of Rights Happily, the times indicate that to create such an order not only is the proper policy of government but it is the only line of safety for our economic structures as well.

We know now that these economic units cannot exist unless prosperity is uniform—that is, unless purchasing power is well distributed throughout every group in the nation.

That is why even the most selfish of corporations for its own interest would be glad to see wages restored and unemployment aided and to bring the Western farmer back to his accustomed level of prosperity and to assure a permanent safety to both groups.

That is why some enlightened industries themselves endeavor to limit the freedom of action of each man and business group within the industry in the common interest of all; why business men everywhere are asking a form of organization which will bring the scheme of things into balance, even though it may in some measure qualify the freedom of action of individual units within the business.

The exposition need not further be elaborated. It is brief and incomplete, but you will be able to expand it in terms of your own business or occupation without difficulty.

I THINK every one who has actually entered the economic struggle—which means every one who was not born to safe wealth—knows in his own experience and his own life that we have now to apply the earlier concepts of American government to the conditions of today.

Social Order Changed

The Declaration of Independence discusses the problem of government in terms of a contract. Government is a relation of give and take—a contract, perforce, if we would follow the thinking out of which it grew.

Under such a contract rulers were accorded power, and the people consented to that power on consideration that they be accorded certain rights.

The task of statesmanship has always been the redefinition of these rights in terms of a changing and growing social order. New conditions impose new requirements upon government and those who conduct government.

I HELD, for example, in proceedings before me as Governor the purpose of which was the removal of the Sheriff of New York, that under modern conditions it was not enough for a public official merely to evade the legal terms of official **Officeholders** wrongdoing.   He owed a positive **Must Be** duty as well. **Frank** I said, in substance, that if he had acquired large sums of money, he was, when accused, required to explain the sources of such wealth.   To that extent this wealth was colored with a public interest.

I said that public servants should, even beyond private citizens, in financial matters be held to a stern and uncompromising rectitude.

I feel that we are coming to a view, through the drift of our legislation and our public thinking in the past quarter century, that private economic power is, to enlarge an old phrase, a public trust as well.

I hold that continued enjoyment of that power by any individual or group must depend upon the fulfillment of that trust.   The men who have reached the summit of American business life know this best; happily, many of these urge the binding quality of this greater social contract.

The terms of that contract are as old as the Republic and as new as the new economic order.

E VERY man has a right to life, and this means that he has also a right to make a comfortable living. He may by sloth or crime decline to exercise that right, but it may not be denied him.

We have no actual famine or **Right to** dearth; our industrial and agricul-**Make Living** tural mechanism can produce enough and to spare.

Our government, formal and informal, political and economic, owes to every one an avenue to possess himself of a portion of that plenty sufficient for his needs through his own work.

Every man has a right to his own property, which means a right to be assured to the fullest extent attainable, in the safety of his savings. By no other means can men carry the burdens of those parts of life which in the nature of things afford no chance of labor—childhood, sickness, old age.

In all thought of property, this right is paramount; all other property rights must yield to it.

If, in accord with this principle, we must restrict the operations of the speculator, the manipulator, even the financier, I believe we must accept the restriction as needful not to hamper individualism but to protect it.

THESE two requirements must be satisfied, in the main, by the individuals who claim and hold control of the great industrial and financial combinations which dominate so large a part of our industrial life.

Must Work Together

They have undertaken to be not business men but princes—princes of property.

I am not prepared to say that the system which produces them is wrong. I am very clear that they must fearlessly and competently assume the responsibility which go with the power. So many enlightened business men know this that the statement would be little more than a platitude were it not for an added implication.

This implication is, briefly, that the responsible heads of finance and industry, instead of acting each for himself, must work together to achieve the common end.

They must, where necessary, sacrifice this or that private advantage, and in reciprocal self-denial must seek a general advantage. It is here that formal government—political government, if you choose—comes in.

WHENEVER in the pursuit of this objective the lone wolf, the unethical competitor, the reckless promoter, the Ishmael or Insull, whose hand is against every man's, declines to join in achieving an end recognized as being for the public welfare, and threatens to drag the industry back to a state of anarchy, the government may properly be asked to apply restraint.

Refers to Insull

Likewise, should the group ever use its collective power contrary to the public welfare, the government must be swift to enter and protect the public interest.

The government should assume the function of economic regulation only as a last resort, to be tried only when private initiative, inspired by high responsibility, with such assistance and balance as government can give, has finally failed.

As yet there has been no final failure, because there has been no attempt; and I decline to assume that this nation is unable to meet the situation.

The final term of the high contract was for liberty and the pursuit of happiness.

We have learned a great deal of both in the past century. We know that individual liberty and individual happiness mean nothing unless both are ordered in the sense that one man's meat is not another man's poison.

We know that the old "rights of personal competency"—the right to read, to think, to speak, to choose and live a mode of life—must be respected at all hazards.

WE know that liberty to do anything which deprives others of those elemental rights is outside the protection of any compact, and that government in this regard is the maintenance of a balance within which every individual may have a place if he will take it, in which every individual may find safety if he wishes it, in which every individ-

Must Maintain Balance

ual may attain such power as his ability permits, consistent with his assuming the accompanying responsibility.

All this is a long, slow task. Nothing is more striking than the simple innocence of the men who insist, whenever an objective is present, on the prompt production of a patent scheme guaranteed to produce a result.

Human endeavor is not so simple as that. Government includes the art of formulating a policy and using the political technique to attain so much of that policy as will receive general support; persuading, leading, sacrificing, teaching always, because the greatest duty of a statesman is to educate.

But in the matters of which I have spoken we are learning rapidly in a severe school. The lessons so learned must not be forgotten even in the mental lethargy of a speculative upturn.

WE must build toward the time when a major depression cannot occur again; and if this means sacrificing the easy profits of inflationist booms, then let them go; and good riddance.

Issues a Warning Faith in America, faith in our tradition of personal responsibility, faith in our institutions, faith in ourselves demands that we recognize the new terms of the old social contact.

We shall fulfill them, as we fulfilled the obligation of the apparent utopia which Jefferson imagined for us in 1776 and which Jefferson, Roosevelt and Wilson sought to bring to realization.

We must do so lest a rising tide of misery, engendered by our common failure, engulf us all.

But failure is not an American habit, and in the strength of great hope we must all shoulder our common load.

JOHN F. KENNEDY

John Fitzgerald Kennedy

Inaugural Address, January 20, 1961

JOHN F. KENNEDY's inaugural address was delivered in snow-clad Washington on January 20, 1961, and was heard by millions of people throughout the United States and elsewhere in the world. Though the president-elect had worked diligently for a month upon his address, he observed characteristically, after rereading Thomas Jefferson's inaugural address of 1801 (page 51), "better than mine."

Several of the new president's ringing statements have already become part of the American heritage: "The world is very different now. For man holds in his mortal hands the power to abolish all forms of human poverty and all forms of human life"; "Let us never negotiate out of fear. But never let us fear to negotiate"; and in the peroration, "Ask not what America can do for you, but what together we can do for the freedom of man." The most famous admonition is, of course, "Ask not what your country can do for you—ask what you can do for your country." This utterance, according to Arthur Schlesinger, Jr., has had a long history and had lain in Kennedy's mind for a long time. Justice Oliver Wendell Holmes had used it in a Memorial Day Address in 1884.

In his address the president expressed the spirit of the postwar generation, summoned America to new exertions and initiatives, and boldly replaced the clichés of the cold war with new challenges. A number of friends and advisers submitted suggestions, and Theodore C. Sorensen, his close associate, contributed to the contents of the address.

The Kennedy "Inaugural Address" was officially printed as Senate Document No. 9, 87th Congress, in session, Government Printing Office, Washington, 1961.

87TH CONGRESS
1st Session

SENATE

DOCUMENT
No. 9

INAUGURAL ADDRESS

OF

John Fitzgerald Kennedy

PRESIDENT OF THE UNITED STATES

DELIVERED AT THE CAPITOL
WASHINGTON, D.C.

JANUARY 20, 1961

U.S. GOVERNMENT PRINTING OFFICE
WASHINGTON : 1961

57011°

SUBMITTED BY MR. MANSFIELD

———

IN THE SENATE OF THE UNITED STATES,
January 23, 1961.

Ordered, That the Inaugural Address of the President of the United States, delivered on Friday, January 20, 1961, be printed as a Senate document.

Attest:

Felton M. Johnston

Secretary, U.S. Senate.

II

INAUGURAL ADDRESS OF PRESIDENT
JOHN FITZGERALD KENNEDY
ON
FRIDAY, JANUARY 20, 1961

Mr. Chief Justice, President Eisenhower, Vice President Nixon, President Truman, reverend clergy, fellow citizens, we observe today not a victory of party, but a celebration of freedom—symbolizing an end, as well as a beginning—signifying renewal, as well as change. For I have sworn before you and Almighty God the same solemn oath our forebears prescribed nearly a century and three quarters ago.

The world is very different now. For man holds in his mortal hands the power to abolish all forms of human poverty and all forms of human life. And yet the same revolutionary beliefs for which our forebears fought are still at issue around the globe—the belief that the rights of man come not from the generosity of the state, but from the hand of God.

We dare not forget today that we are the heirs of that first revolution. Let the word go forth from this time and place, to friend and foe alike, that the torch has been passed to a new generation of Americans—born in this century, tempered by war, disciplined by a hard and bitter peace, proud of our ancient heritage—and unwilling to witness or permit the slow undoing of those human rights to which this Nation has always been committed, and to which we are committed today at home and around the world.

Let every nation know, whether it wishes us well or ill, that we shall pay any price, bear any burden, meet any hardship, support any friend, oppose any foe, in order to assure the survival and the success of liberty.

This much we pledge—and more.

To those old allies whose cultural and spiritual origins we share, we pledge the loyalty of faithful friends. United, there is little we cannot do in a host of cooperative ventures. Divided, there is little we can do—for we dare not meet a powerful challenge at odds and split asunder.

To those new States whom we welcome to the ranks of the free, we pledge our words that one form of colonial control shall not have passed away merely to be replaced by a far greater iron tyranny. We shall not always expect to find them supporting our view. But we shall always hope to find them strongly supporting their own freedom—and to remember that, in the past, those who foolishly sought power by riding the back of the tiger ended up inside.

To those peoples in the huts and villages across the globe struggling to break the bonds of mass misery, we pledge our best efforts to help them help themselves, for whatever period is required—not because the Communists may be doing it, not because we seek their votes,

INAUGURAL ADDRESS OF JOHN FITZGERALD KENNEDY

but because it is right. If a free society cannot help the many who are poor, it cannot save the few who are rich.

To our sister republics south of our border, we offer a special pledge—to convert our good words into good deeds, in a new alliance for progress, to assist free men and free governments in casting off the chains of poverty. But this peaceful revolution of hope cannot become the prey of hostile powers. Let all our neighbors know that we shall join with them to oppose aggression or subversion anywhere in the Americas. And let every other power know that this hemisphere intends to remain the master of its own house.

To that world assembly of sovereign states, the United Nations, our last best hope in an age where the instruments of war have far outpaced the instruments of peace, we renew our pledge of support—to prevent it from becoming merely a forum for invective—to strengthen its shield of the new and the weak—and to enlarge the area in which its writ may run.

Finally, to those nations who would make themselves our adversary, we offer not a pledge but a request: that both sides begin anew the quest for peace, before the dark powers of destruction unleashed by science engulf all humanity in planned or accidental self-destruction.

We dare not tempt them with weakness. For only when our arms are sufficient beyond doubt can we be certain beyond doubt that they will never be employed.

But neither can two great and powerful groups of nations take comfort from our present course—both sides overburdened by the cost of modern weapons, both rightly alarmed by the steady spread of the deadly atom, yet both racing to alter that uncertain balance of terror that stays the hand of mankind's final war.

So let us begin anew—remembering on both sides that civility is not a sign of weakness, and sincerity is always subject to proof. **Let us never negotiate out of fear. But let us never fear to negotiate.**

Let both sides explore what problems unite us instead of laboring those problems which divide us.

Let both sides, for the first time, formulate serious and precise proposals for the inspection and control of arms—and bring the absolute power to destroy other nations under the absolute control of all nations.

Let both sides seek to invoke the wonders of science instead of its terrors. Together let us explore the stars, conquer the deserts, eradicate disease, tap the ocean depths, and encourage the arts and commerce.

Let both sides unite to heed in all corners of the earth the command of Isaiah—to "undo the heavy burdens and to let the oppressed go free."

And if a beachhead of cooperation may push back the jungle of suspicion, let both sides join in creating a new endeavor, not a new balance of power, but a new world of law, where the strong are just and the weak secure and the peace preserved.

All this will not be finished in the first 100 days. Nor will it be finished in the first 1,000 days, nor in the life of this administration, nor even perhaps in our lifetime on this planet. But let us begin.

INAUGURAL ADDRESS OF JOHN FITZGERALD KENNEDY

In your hands, my fellow citizens, more than in mine, will rest the final success or failure of our course. Since this country was founded, each generation of Americans has been summoned to give testimony to its national loyalty. The graves of young Americans who answered the call to service are found around the globe.

Now the trumpet summons us again—not as a call to bear arms, though arms we need; not as a call to battle, though embattled we are; but a call to bear the burden of a long twilight struggle, year in, and year out, "rejoicing in hope, patient in tribulation"—a struggle against the common enemies of man: tyranny, poverty, disease, and war itself.

Can we forge against these enemies a grand and global alliance, North and South, East and West, that can assure a more fruitful life for all mankind? Will you join in that historic effort?

In the long history of the world, only a few generations have been granted the role of defending freedom in its hour of maximum danger. I do not shrink from this responsibility—I welcome it. I do not believe that any of us would exchange places with any other people or any other generation. The energy, the faith, the devotion which we bring to this endeavor will light our country and all who serve it—and the glow from that fire can truly light the world.

And so, my fellow Americans, ask not what your country can do for you: Ask what you can do for your country.

My fellow citizens of the world: Ask not what America will do for you, but what together we can do for the freedom of man.

Finally, whether you are citizens of America or citizens of the world, ask of us the same high standards of strength and sacrifice which we ask of you. With a good conscience our only sure reward, with history the final judge of our deeds, let us go forth to lead the land we love, asking His blessing and His help, but knowing that here on earth God's work must truly be our own.

O